EXTRAORDINARY
PRAYER

DAILY PRAYERS FOR ALL OCCASIONS

AL MOZINGO

Extraordinary Prayer

Copyright © 2021 by Al Mozingo All rights reserved.

No part of this publication may be reproduced, stored in a retrieval system or transmitted in any way by any means, electronic, mechanical, photocopy, recording or otherwise without the prior permission of the author except as provided by USA copyright law.

The opinions expressed by the author are not necessarily those of URLink Print and Media.

1603 Capitol Ave., Suite 310 Cheyenne, Wyoming USA 82001
1-888-980-6523 | admin@urlinkpublishing.com

URLink Print and Media is committed to excellence in the publishing industry.

Book design copyright © 2021 by URLink Print and Media. All rights reserved.

Published in the United States of America

Library of Congress Control Number: 2021900640
ISBN 978-1-64753-636-7 (Paperback)
ISBN 978-1-64753-637-4 (Digital)

20.11.20

TABLE OF CONTENTS

Introduction v

1) What is Prayer? 1
2) Acquire the Gift of Prayer 3
3) Simplified Prayer 8
4) Church Prayers 13
5) Prayers From Within 16
6) Poems From Within 20
7) Complex Prayers 43
8) Monthly Intercessory Prayer 67
   - *January Intercessory Prayer* 68
   - *February Intercessory Prayer* 69
   - *March Intercessory Prayer* 70
   - *April Intercessory Prayer* 71
   - *May Intercessory Prayer* 72
   - *June Intercessory Prayer* 73
   - *July Intercessory Prayer* 74
   - *August Intercessory Prayer* 75
   - *September Intercessory Prayer* 76
   - *October Intercessory Prayer* 77
   - *November Intercessory Prayer* 78
   - *December Intercessory Prayer* 79

9)	Prayers From Saints	80
10)	Chaplain Prayers	86
	10a) *Christian Prayers*	87
	10b) *Catholic Prayers*	94
	10c) *Mormon*	104
	10d) *Unitarian*	105
	10e) *Jehovah Witnesses*	106
	10f) *Jewish Prayers*	107
	10g) *Islam, Muslim Prayers*	108
	10h) *Buddhism*	109
	10i) *Hinduism*	111
11)	The Lord's Prayer	113

Appendix A (*How To Improve Your Prayer Life*) 119
Appendix B (*The Imitation of Christ*) 121
Appendix C (*Favorite Scriptures*) 123

References 135

We start our day,
we begin to pray.

INTRODUCTION

The creation of this book began years ago when I first became a Christian. I found I had a heart for praying, first for myself, and then for others. This brought me closer to God. With the help of God, I have changed my prayer life as my relationship with God has become closer. My heart has opened to his call and incorporating his Spirit within; which has led me to an active prayer life.

Prayers that I have used, that mean so much to me, I started saving them to memory and then wrote them in my notebook. It has been many years now as I aspire to be a humble servant. I attempt to imitate Jesus Christ my Lord and Savior and expand my interior life in prayer. With the help of the Holy Spirit I have changed from a man looking to have God make things the way I want; to a man searching God's heart and asking him for his will to be done.

Leading Bible Studies, becoming a Retreat Leader, and a Director of Christian Initiation at church are just a few of the many ministries I have participated in that brought me to extend my prayer life. The Holy Spirit revealed to me the needs of his children and showed me more of what's on his heart. I have had others tell me, "you should write a book of your prayers!" Many of my prayers and poems were given to me while sleeping through dreams and are recorded in my notebook. Through my spiritual growth, love of God, and others I was inspired to write.

I progressed into becoming a Chaplain, attending two different Chaplain Academies. I had my choice, to work with a Sheriff's Department or a Hospital after finishing the academies. I became a Chaplain at a hospital and committed myself to helping the sick and people in need. As a Chaplain, I began to put together several prayers I could use in that position. As a Chaplain you encounter many different religions and beliefs. I was called to pray for others, to provide them peace and consolation as a Volunteer Chaplain.

After several years I was asked by a Pastor to write a book of prayers. I realized that the Holy Spirit had led me to compile a book, with several people asking me to write prayers down over the years. Those multiple confirmations have led me to this point where I started putting pen-to-paper. I have written hundreds of religious articles over the years, so I have been well prepared to write and publish "Extraordinary Prayers." This book includes those inspired prayers of my own, which are conversations with God. This book took over 30 years to write.

~ May you find these prayers a blessing and comfort as I have. ~

Al Mozingo

WHAT IS PRAYER?

I define it as communication with God; raising our heart, mind and soul with an earnest hope in God. It can be done in a variety of forms: praising God, worshiping God, thanking God, asking God for something, and intercession for others. There are many ways to define prayer – this book will help one to see the various ways to describe prayer. The one thing that they all contain, is raising your heart, mind and soul to God. Most of what I write is oriented with the Christian view point. However, I know there are many other beliefs and many thoughts of what prayer is, but they are all to communicate to their Supreme Being.

Prayer conveys our humanity with our suffering through our adversity, tribulations in which we vent our inner pain, sorrow, and negative feelings; we also express our positive feelings of desires, hopes, dreams, faith, and love to God. Searching for God's wisdom, understanding, and most of all his will for ourselves and happiness in God.

Prayer is our love to God and his love to us. God wants to be with us always and wants us to want to be with him; so, he is always waiting for you as a loving parent would. We are his sons and daughters and he always is there for us. God is content just sitting quietly with you in his presence. We don't need to have something to say, be content to feel the eternal love he has for you. Always know whatever you are doing or thinking, he is right there with you. He is showing you answers which is elevating our thoughts and love to his. This is done while leaving you freely to choose your own wants or his. He loves us no matter what we do, right or wrong. Our free will is always our free will. He hopes our will is aligned with him in unity. God doesn't change, it is only us that change.

Realize he is there for us in every decision and thought we make. So, if we feel lost and can't figure something out, ask for God's grace to show us the way. Talk to him as a friend, that is where he wants to be. After all, that is why he created you, to be close and personal, and share everything with you; as seen in the relationship with God the Father and Jesus his Son.

Another thought –
We can also pray to others for their intercession for they too want and must follow God's will, here below is an example:

'Angel of God, my guardian dear, to who God's love commits me here, ever this day be at my side, to light and guard, to rule and guide. Amen.'

2

ACQUIRE THE GIFT OF PRAYER

If you wish to preserve or acquire the gift of prayer, keep yourself connected by making frequent aspirations to God and keep him in your heart.[1]

Why Do We Pray?

Prayer is to direct our mind to God; all it is, is talking to him. Just like how you talk to friends, or tell your family what's going on in your life. God wants to help you find peace in your urgency. We do that in the following ways:

- ➢ We ask God to direct our path to one of holiness, to his holy will.
- ➢ We ask God to infuse us with faith, hope, and love.
- ➢ We ask God to help develop our spiritual life into a deep spirituality, a deep conversion, a deep holiness.
- ➢ We praise God with all our heart, soul, mind, and strength.
- ➢ We ask God to infuse us with his love, to help our love for one another.
- ➢ We ask God to strengthen our hearts and minds.
- ➢ We ask God to give us grace to endure the challenges of life.

- ➢ We ask God to give us the knowledge and wisdom to know his will.
- ➢ We finally ask God for the gift of entering in heaven with him forever and ever.
- ➢ We pray to be transformed into the heart of Christ.

When we finish, we pray to the Father, through the Son Jesus Christ, and in the Holy Spirit. Amen.

Another aspect of why we pray is Intercessory Prayer or praying for others.

Now let us look at some simplified prayers! Some of these phrases can be used as affirmations in our own personal relation to God. They can be used to help us in our beliefs and to help us keep God on our mind. Some of them I have developed in my heart and I wrote them down here; others were in the daily readings as a responsorial from the Psalms of the Bible.[2]

The Way to Prayer

The simplest prayer, yet so many misunderstand. When you love someone, you just want to be near them. We look at them and they look at us, and that is a comfort and pleasure you feel, knowing God is with you and you are with him. Another way, we could say, 'we rest in God.' That is the simplest of prayers, and so meaningful. When we have things to say, we tell God we need him, we want him, or we love him. We express our gratitude to God for everything we have. We praise the Lord for his goodness and love. We ask God for something we need, we want, or we hope for. How do we do this? It takes many forms:

- ➢ Dancing before God. *(King David)*
- ➢ Marching around in a circle. *(Jericho)*

- ➤ Looking at God's creation, *(See it in Wonder)*
- ➤ Laughing for God's Goodness and Love. *(Joyful)*
- ➤ Kneeling before the Lord. *(Adoration)*
- ➤ Saying the name of Jesus. *(Acknowledging)*
- ➤ Sitting in silence. *(Listening to the Holy Spirit)*
- ➤ Talking to God like a friend. *(Conversing with God)*
- ➤ Reading a structured or traditional prayer. *(Bible)*
- ➤ Expressing ourself for a need, want, or desire. *(God)*[1]
- ➤ *Add your own, only you can express you! (Be yourself)*

Different Types of Prayer

1. **Friendly and loving conversation** with the creator. He wants to share with you and he wants you to share with him.
2. **Vocal prayer** is saying a prayer out loud with your voice. When we speak aloud, we can hear our prayer. It is proclaiming to God our creator. It also may help provide you with comfort; stating, singing, yelling, crying or laughing. Confirming your intent and help establish your fortitude.
3. **Internal or mental prayer** is saying the prayer within one's mind. This helps you affirm your prayer of thought and wonder. Help you contemplate and mold your inner feelings; it also, helps develop what you are thinking, prioritizing ideas of your heart, mind and soul. It will help you bring about the full intention of the prayer to your creator God. God is there in your conscience; he watches and reveals what he would suggest. This quiet prayer helps it ascend to God. Now you have registered your feelings more clearly about how you actually think and feel. Continued prayer like this leads further towards meditation and contemplative prayer.

4. **Simple prayer** is just using a few words to raise your heart and mind towards God. In many ways, this gives the mind pause from whatever activity or thought you are in. This brings you for a moment to share and acknowledge what you are thinking to God.
5. **Complex prayer** is using multiple thoughts and aspects of spirituality to raise your heart and mind towards God. Our mind thinks of so many things at one time. When we have so many things we are thinking about, we need to organize them so that we can understand what we are praying for. God doesn't need this, but we do. We need to be fully aware of what we say and share what exactly we want. Sometimes if it is too complex, I suggest writing it down so that we can say it correctly and make sense to ourselves, especially if you are praying with someone else or a group. When praying for others, write them down so that names and intentions are correct. This may focus purpose and meaning of the prayer more clearly.

6. **Meditation** is a prayer of reflection, when we use our intellect to think about what something means to us. Reflect on a word or experience or just on God alone. Meditating on something you are pondering to increase your understanding of it. When in this meditative state, you are looking to define what you think or feel while sharing it with God, as you discover his way, truth, and life.
7. **Contemplation** is a prayer taking one's mind to a higher level, it is when we focus our body, mind and spirit toward God. We are in essence, resting in God.

Only you, my Savior, can give peace to my soul, because you were the mediator of peace between your eternal Father and us. Dear Jesus, calm the storms that reign in my heart. Help me to do your holy will in everything, that I may live in true peace and perfect calm. Amen.

SIMPLIFIED PRAYER

Simplified Prayers

Saying daily prayer(s) repeatedly throughout the day helps focus one's mind on God and it will assist in bringing you closer to God while dwelling on him. I choose a simplified prayer that fits my heart at that present time. I always try to stay upbeat through tribulations and periods of suffering, knowing that God turns all things to good and he protects me from all things that are too much for me to bare. Below are examples of simplified prayers:

- † God is love.
- † Love surrounds me.
- † Jesus is Lord.
- † God is my refuge.
- † God's grace is enough.
- † I praise you Lord Jesus Christ.
- † I will sing in God's presence.
- † Holy, holy, holy Lord.
- † I come to do your will Lord.
- † I will sing about your salvation.
- † I have my hope in you Lord.
- † God is my rock and my salvation.

- ✝ The Lord is kind and merciful.
- ✝ I proclaim your goodness.
- ✝ Blessed are they who hope in God.
- ✝ Serve God and others.
- ✝ I will praise you forever God.
- ✝ God is within me.
- ✝ Guide me Lord.
- ✝ The Lord's kindness is everlasting.
- ✝ Lord I give you thanks for all things.
- ✝ Lord help me to reflect on your love.
- ✝ Rejoice in the Lord.
- ✝ God's mercy is overflowing.
- ✝ Trust in God's goodness and love.
- ✝ God, have mercy on me.
- ✝ Jesus, I trust in you.
- ✝ Be reconciled to God.
- ✝ We are ambassadors for Christ.
- ✝ Now is the day of salvation.
- ✝ Jesus is Lord.
- ✝ Love surrounds me.
- ✝ Show love always.
- ✝ God alone.
- ✝ Happiness is found in the Lord.
- ✝ Praise the Lord.
- ✝ Eternal life is a gift from God.
- ✝ Rest in the Lord.
- ✝ Give honor and glory to God.
- ✝ Be with me Lord.
- ✝ Your words are spirit and life.
- ✝ Jesus help me grow in holiness.
- ✝ God give me the grace to show love.
- ✝ I give glory and honor to you O Lord.

- † Jesus is the Alpha and the Omega.
- † Jesus is God's true light.
- † Jesus is the word of God.
- † Our ultimate goal is union with God.
- † Thank you, Jesus.
- † I love you Jesus.
- † I praise you Jesus.
- † Take over my life Lord.
- † God is my shield.
- † Lord protect me in your love.
- † Come, Holy Spirit.
- † God is the author of all things.
- † God have compassion on me.
- † Christ is my rock.
- † The Lord is gracious and merciful.
- † O God I come to do your will.
- † I love you Jesus with all my heart.
- † I open my heart to you today.
- † I humble myself to you God almighty.
- † The words of mercy are from God.
- † God, all that I have is from you Lord.
- † Glorify the Lord.
- † Taste and see the glory of the Lord.
- † I praise you Lord.
- † Happiness and joy are from the Lord.
- † The Lord is with me.
- † Lord, heal me.
- † The Lord is love.
- † O Lord hear my prayer.
- † God comforts me.
- † God is present in me.
- † I am filled with joy.

† The Lord has done great things.
† A sing to you O Lord.
† Almighty Father.
† O God you are king of the universe.
† His love endures forever.
† God is great – all the time.
† I love you God.
† God, I give you glory and praise.
† I call upon the Lord.
† The Lord is with me.
† God will turn our mourning into joy.
† The Lord guards us.
† The Lord is my light and salvation.
† Lord in your great love answer me.
† I seek the Lord with all my heart.
† Surrender to God today.
† Lord you bring me peace.
† Rejoice, in the Lord.
† Jesus is the cornerstone.
† God's love is everlasting.
† The Lord hears the cry of the poor.
† Believe in Jesus.
† Holy Spirit, lead me.
† I meditate on your love God.
† My prayer to God is powerful.
† I will sing the goodness of the Lord.
† I praise your name forever O God.
† I'm after God's own heart.
† I give you thanks O Lord.
† Lord send out your spirit.
† Lord renew the face of the earth.
† Holy is the Lord our God.

- ✝ The glory of the Lord is within.
- ✝ My God, I give you thanks.
- ✝ Let your face shine upon me.
- ✝ Hide me in the shelter of your love.
- ✝ Lord, you are my rock and fortress.
- ✝ I rejoice in your love O Lord.
- ✝ Lord, I take refuge in you.
- ✝ I am a light to others.
- ✝ I help inspire and encourage others.
- ✝ I Give Jesus my heart.
- ✝ I have an attitude of gratitude.

Pray without ceasing. *(1 Thess 5:17)*

CHURCH PRAYERS

There are more than 40,000 different Christian Church denominations. There are so many more prayers, that come from the hearts of humanity. These are some of the Christian church prayers I am familiar with:

Thanksgiving for the Day
This is the day the Lord has made; let us rejoice in it and be glad. Amen.[3]

Genuine Sorrow
O God, be merciful to me a sinner. Amen.[4]

Morning Prayer
In the name of our Lord Jesus Christ I will begin this day. I thank you, Lord, for having preserved me during the night. I will do my best to make all I do today pleasing to you and in accordance with your will.

Love
Heavenly Father help me to love my neighbor as myself. Amen.[5]

Forgiveness
Father give me the grace to forgive others, so you heavenly Father will forgive me. Amen.[6]

Come Holy Spirit
Come Holy Spirit, fill the hearts of your faithful and kindle in them the fire of your love. Send forth your Spirit to renew the face of the earth. Amen.

Glory Be *(Doxology)*
Glory be to the Father and to the Son and to the Holy Spirit, as it was in the beginning is now, and ever shall be world without end. Amen.

Give Us This Day Our Daily Bread
Give us this day our daily bread, we ask you God for our daily subsistence. In Jesus Christ our Lord and Savior. Amen.

The Shepherd *(Cf. Ps 23)*
The Lord is my shepherd; I shall not want. He leads me and guides me in the path of righteousness. Even though I walk through the valley of death I will fear no evil; for goodness and love shall follow me all the days of my life. And I will dwell in the house of the Lord forever. Amen.

Your Will Be Done
Heavenly Father, I pray to you with a humble heart. I pray not my will, but yours be done.[7] I pray that I conform myself to your will and that I no longer live, but Christ lives in me. Amen.[8]

Angels to Guard you
God command your angels to guard me wherever I go.[9]

Call Jesus
I call on you Lord Jesus save me.[10]

Jesus Guide Me
Jesus, Jesus, Jesus, come to me and be with me Lord, guide me through my troubles.

Jesus is Lord
O God, for I confess with my mouth that Jesus is Lord and believe in my heart that God raised Jesus from the dead, save me. Amen.[11]

God Loves the World
My God I know that you love us so much, that you gave us your only begotten Son, so that we who believe might have eternal life. Amen.[12]

Prayer Before Study
Ineffable Creator, you are called the true font of light and wisdom, and the origin of all things. Pour forth a ray of your brightness into the darkened places of my mind; disperse from my soul the twofold darkness into which I was born, sin and ignorance.

Grant me keenness of mind, capacity to remember, skill in learning, insight to interpret, and eloquence in speech.

May you guide the beginning of my study, direct its progress, and bring it to completion. Through Christ our Lord. Amen.[13]

PRAYERS FROM WITHIN

The following are some prayers I have written over the years; inspired within me, by the Holy Spirit.

Prayers for Family and Friends

Almighty Father I come to you in prayer with a humble heart. Father I ask for your forgiveness for any sins I have committed; in my thoughts, words, and deeds; in what I have done and what I failed to do. Father I pray for your mercy and grace for myself, my family, and my friends. I pray that we all have health, happiness, and a long life. May we be infused with faith, hope, and love. May we have patience, peace, and joy in life. May we all be transformed; may we all develop a deep spirituality, a deep conversion, a deep holiness, toward the Father, Son and Holy Spirit. Father, give us grace to endure the challenges of life. Father, at life's end allow me to say: Into your hands I commend my spirit. Father, at life's end may you say: Well done good and faithful servant. Father at life's end allow me to enter into heaven with you forever and ever. I pray this to God the Father, through Jesus Christ, in the Holy Spirit; with Mary the Mother of God, my Guardian Angel, and in Communion with all the Angels and Saints. To you Almighty Father be the glory forever and ever. Amen.

A Prayer for Peace

Almighty Father, I know for you nothing is impossible. I ask for a very specific prayer: Give me peace! I want the joy and happiness you have ready for anyone who follows you. I want the joy and happiness you have ready for myself and my family. I know there is nothing in this world that can give me true joy, happiness, and peace. you are my joy and my happiness. I rest in you, with all my love. I am at peace when resting in you. Amen.

A Prayer for Holiness

Heavenly Father, I pray to live a life you want me to live. I pray that you send the Holy Spirit to live within me; to lead me and to guide me to righteousness. I want to do your will; I want to say I live no longer, but Christ lives within me. I want to be holy as you are holy. Give me your mercy when I fail. Give me your grace in the challenges of life. Give me your love, patience, and holiness. I pray in Jesus Christ my Lord and Savior. Amen.

A Change of heart

Heavenly Father, I pray that you free us from our hearts of stone. We might even have anger and hatred. We might even hold grudges, with un-forgiveness in our heart. We need to change!

Father help us to obtain the virtues needed to be more holy. We ask you Father for the following virtues: A loving caring heart, a heart that shows kindness, a heart of forgiveness, a heart of compassion, a heart led by the Holy Spirit, a heart led by example from Jesus, and a heart full of love. Amen.

A Prayer for Bible Study

Heavenly Father, open our hearts and minds to your word. Help us to see your goodness and love. Speak to us through your words, to know you, to love you, and to serve you. Enlighten us through your knowledge. Give us the grace to understand your ways. Endow upon us with your wisdom. Increase our faith, hope, and love. Through Jesus Christ in the Holy Spirit we pray. Amen.

Transformative Love

Heavenly Father, help me to show other's your love, through my humility, kindness, forgiveness, mercy, compassion, patience, and generosity. This transformative love is from you O God that springs up from within me. This transformative love is found from following Jesus' the way, the truth, and the life. This transformative love is lived out through my openness to others in thought, word, and deed. Amen.[14]

A Prayer for Travelers

Almighty and merciful God, who commissioned thy angels to guide and protect us. Father, command them to be our companions on our journey. Clothe us with invisible protection, to keep us from all dangers; of collision, of fire, of explosion, and of any injury. Finally, preserve us from all evil especially from sin; to guide us to our heavenly home. Through Jesus Christ our Lord and the Holy Spirit. Amen.

Now I See!

Heavenly Father I pray; I was blind and now I see; because I opened my heart to Jesus. I know you love me unconditionally. you sent your only begotten Son from heaven to save us from sin and death. Christ brought us, the "Good News," your love and mercy. Our believing in this and following Jesus made us children of God. Thank you, for your son Jesus; when he rose from the dead, he sent us the Holy Spirit. Now, I have faith, hope, and love given to me as a gift. Now I live a life of grace, a better life; exhibiting mercy, respect and love to others. I have begun to believe in a life eternal in heaven with you Father. I know I have been reconciled with you Father, by the sacrifice of your Son Jesus Christ. Now I can say: "Jesus, I trust in you." Now I See! In Jesus' name I pray. Amen.

Serenity Prayer

God, grant me the serenity to accept the things I cannot change, courage to change the things I can, and wisdom to know the difference.[15]

Cry out to the Lord from your heart. *(Lam 2:18)*

6

POEMS FROM WITHIN

The following are some poems I have written over the years; inspired within me by the Holy Spirit. I believe you can use a poem as prayer. Just say "Amen" at the end of the reading of the poem. Also note some of the poems have references from scripture; that were used to inspire me on the writing of the poem.

Free Will

Lord I want to love you
Lord I want to love others
Lord I want to show goodness
Lord I want to show forgiveness

Lord I want to be free from sin
Lord I want to be free from hate
Lord I want to have hope
Lord I want to have joy

Lord I want to follow you
Lord I want to do your will
Lord I want to serve you
Lord I want to obey you

Lord I am free to show your love
Lord I am free to show your forgiveness
Lord I am free to show your peace
Lord I am free to show your light

Your Witness Proclaimed

Let Christ within be seen today!
Let Christ' love emanate from you

Show Christ' generosity in your actions
Show Christ' forgiveness in your actions

Share Christ' love through your love
Share Christ' love through your service

Witness Christ' miracles in your interactions
Witness Christ' transformation in your life

A Cry to God

Save me O God,
I have sunk into the depths of despair

Save me O God
I am weary and cry out in pain

Save me O God
I have lost my strength and I am hurt

Save me O God
I have sinned and I am ashamed

Help me O God
Rescue me from the depths of despair

Help me O God
Rescue me from my weariness and pain

Help me O God
Rescue me from weakness and hurt

Help me O God
Rescue me from my sinfulness

Thankyou O God,
for bringing me out of the depths of despair

A Grateful Heart

I praise your holy name Lord
I exalt you over all others Lord
I thank you Lord with all my heart

Lord you strengthen my spirit
Lord I love to hear your holy word
Lord how great is your glory

The Lord cares for the lowly
The Lord saves me and loves me
The Lord is with me forever and ever[16]

A Moment in Time

A thousand years in your eyes Lord
Is but a moment in time O God

We are here today and gone tomorrow
Watch over us O God

We are but mortals returning to dust
May we live with you for eternity O God

We have faults and are sinful people
Forgive us for our sins O God

Our years are short, seventy or eighty
May we live a long fruitful life O God

Help us in this life with mercy and grace
Bless us with happiness O God

Teach us to count our days
May we obtain wisdom of heart O God

Help us to praise you always
Fill us with your holy love O God

We humble, ourselves to you Lord
We are servants to do your will O God

A thousand years in your eyes Lord
Favor me that moment in time O God[17]

Perseverance and Prayer

Believing in Jesus doesn't shield you
Hardships will come your way

Pray for God's grace to love
Pray for the ability to forgive others

Pray to persevere the challenges of life
Pray to overcome any fears within you

Pray that you are not disturbed by worldly things
Pray that God helps you through your tribulations

Jesus is alive and loves all of us forever and ever
Jesus says, "love one another as I have loved you."

You must be patient and make your hearts firm,
Because the coming of the Lord is at hand.[18]

Lord, my only desire is to know that I am in the state of grace. Please keep me in this state of grace until I die. Pardon all my sin and grant me the grace of perseverance. Amen

Changing Anger to Love

Recognize you are angry, but don't reveal it.
Dismiss anger for peace with patience and love.
Say within "All things are possible with God."

Strive for understanding, peace, and forgiveness.
Strive for love, joy, and peace.
Say within "All things are possible with God."

Strive for more faith, hope, and love.
Strive for God to give you grace to change your heart.
Say within "All things are possible with God."

A Prayer for Divine Favor (cf. Ps 85)

O Lord, restore our good fortune

O Lord, forgive us, your people

O Lord, pardon all of our sins

O Lord, abandon your anger

O Lord, give us life to its fullest

O Lord, we will listen to your word

O Lord, grant us your salvation

O Lord, give us prosperity

O Lord, show us your love

I Am at Peace

I am at peace during stressful times

I am at peace during chaos

I am at peace when I am angry

I am at peace when I am in pain

I am at peace during distress

I am at peace during illness

I am at peace not because of who I am,

I am at peace because of whose I am

Lord, may my heart, which was created by you and for you, love only you and seek only you in all things. With humility I ask you for this love so that I may find rest in you and peace eternally. Amen.

The Clouds of Love

As the clouds move over the land
    They tend to change the light to darkness
The clouds are us moving through life
    The darkness is our sorrow & loneliness
But, just as the clouds give way to light
    So does our sorrow give way to joy
Just as we change from day to day in life
    So does our sorrow change to joy

At times we need the clouds and the rain
    So, we pray at times for the rain
Our sorrow is changed with a contrite heart
    So, we pray for a heart of love & joy
When we find love, we want to hold on to it
    But it moves like the clouds from our reach
So, we reach for someone to love in life
    And we pray for the love of our life
As the light shines and overtakes the clouds
    So too does love overtake our loneliness
We live from day to day with hope
    And we pray day after day for love & joy

Love can come and love can go
    But our prayers are for it to come and stay
True love is what we want in our life
    As rain washes the land clean
So does God's love wash our hearts with joy & peace
    We have faith and we found our love
We have found the love of all life!

Ancient Wisdom

Ancient wisdom can be
    Found in ancient writings

True wisdom is
    Found in Scriptures

Ancient wisdom can be
    Found in classical writings

True wisdom is
    Found in God alone

The Presence of God

My soul is touched by God

My life is sustained by God

My emotions are stirred by God

My spirit is encouraged by God

My physical body is graced by God

My prayers are answered by God

My faith, hope and love are from God

Friendship

Friendship is like a Sunrise
    Beautiful and Warm

Friendship is like Ocean Waves
    Constant and Enduring

Friendship is like a Strong Tree
    Sheltering and Protecting

Friendship is like a Mountain
    Expansive and Strong

Friendship is like the Son
    Sharing and Caring

Harmony

The harmony of song is
    Joy to the soul

The harmony of two people is
    Peace for the two

The harmony of nature is
    Light to the world

The harmony of love is
    Music for the heart

Love

It started as a small flame
It grew rapidly like a great bonfire
Did it grow too rapidly?

What Happened? It started to die!
It needs something to keep the flame burning
Love needs patience and kindness

Love needs good communication
Love is doing unto other as,
you would have them do unto you.

The flame can continue, it burns on
But it needs help, or it dies out.

Fidelity to God

We need to listen to God's word
God asks that we obey him

We understand that God tests us
God wants our obedience

We call out to God in our distress
God hears us when we call

We ask for God to rescue us
God will answer us

We want to walk in God's holy ways
God will help us along the path[19]

Jesus the Suffering Servant

Jesus a man of suffering
He bore our pain
He endured our suffering

He was pierced for our sins
He was crucified for our iniquity
He bore our punishment

He healed us by his wounds
He helps us from going astray
He bore our guilt

He was struck for our sins
He was a reparation offering for us
He surrendered himself to justify us

He interceded for our transgressions
He is our Lord and Savior
He is the Son the Father[20]

> Give me strength, my Savior,
> to imitate you in bearing my cross.

Trinity Prayer

O heavenly Father Creator of the Universe;
I ask to be filled with thy holy love.

O Jesus Christ my Holy Savior;
I ask to be filled with thy holy grace.

O Holy Spirit my Holy Guide;
I ask to be filled with thy holy guidance.

O Holy Trinity I ask for a deep faith within;
I ask to be filled with faith, hope, and love.

O Holy Trinity I ask for a deep spirituality within;
I ask to be filled with your holy wisdom.

O Holy Trinity I ask for a deep holiness within;
I ask to be filled with the desire to love and serve you.

O Holy Trinity I ask for your holy light;
I ask to be filled with the desire to do thy will.

O Holy Trinity I ask for your very essence;
I ask to be filled with the ability to bring others to you.

O Holy Trinity I ask for your very power;
I ask to become one with you forever and ever.

A Simple Prayer

I thank you Father for everything,
I pray to you God with all my heart.

I ask to be guided by the Holy Spirit,
I look for your guidance God.

I study your Holy Word God,
I learn of your goodness and love God.

I profess "Jesus is Lord,"
I ask you to bless me Father.

I pray this in the name of the Father,
Son, and Holy Spirit. Amen.

O God, thank you for my life.

A Song of Love

O heavenly Father I love you
Jesus and the Holy Spirit

I give you my heart and love
Give me your heart and love

I pray to you day and night
Please listen to my prayers

I repent and ask for forgiveness
Forgive me of all my sinfulness

I thank you for sending me your Son
Let his grace dwell within me

I want to become closer to you O God
Send the Holy Spirit to lead me

I thank you for Jesus my Lord and Savior
Please let me dwell with you forever and ever

Amen.

Grant, O God, that I may always love you.

Almighty Father, King of The Universe

We ask for your guidance and grace
    Almighty Father

We thank you for your love and mercy
    Almighty Father

We ask for your help each day
    Almighty Father

We thank you for your Son Jesus Christ
    Almighty Father

We ask for you to allow us to be your light
    Almighty Father

We give you all honor and glory forever Almighty Father,
With the Holy Spirit, Through Jesus Christ your Son. Amen.

Almighty God, lover of the faithful.

Lord Purify My Mind and Heart

Lord Purify My Mind and Heart
    Into thy Holy Will

Lord Purify My Mind and Heart
    Into thy Instrument of Peace

Lord Purify My Mind and Heart
    Into thy Light of Love

Lord Purify My Mind and Heart
    Into thy Mercy and Grace

Lord Purify My Mind and Heart
    Into thy Hope and Joy

Lord Purify My Mind and Heart
    Into thy Consuming Faith

Lord Purify My Mind and Heart
    Into thy Holy Forgiveness

Lord Purify My Mind and Heart
    Into thy Holy Will

Attitude

The Lord is your confidence
Amen.

Do good to others always
Amen.

Help others whenever possible
Amen.

Live in peace with everyone
Amen.

Do not quarrel with others
Amen.

Do not envy others
Amen.

God will show you kindness
Amen.

The Lord blesses the humble
Amen[21]

Bless the Lord

May I praise the Lord with my mouth
    Bless the Lord

May I magnify the Lord in my heart
    Bless the Lord

May I hear the Lord in my soul
    Bless the Lord

May I exalt the Lord's name to the world
    Bless the Lord

May I be delivered by the Lord from my fears
    Bless the Lord

May I be radiant with the Lord's joy in my life
    Bless the Lord

May I be saved by the Lord from distress
    Bless the Lord

May I take refuge in the Lord always
    Bless the Lord

May I receive goodness from the Lord
    Bless the Lord[22]

His Love Endures Forever

I give thanks to the Lord
    His love endures forever

The Lord our God is good
    His love endures forever

I call out to the Lord in distress
    His love endures forever

The Lord our God answers prayers
    His love endures forever

The Lord frees me from sinfulness
    His love endures forever

I have the Lord at my side
    His love endures forever

I have the Lord, I do not fear
    His love endures forever

The Lord our God is my helper
    His love endures forever

I take refuge in the Lord
    His love endures forever

I give thanks to the Lord
    His love endures forever[23]

How Great is Our God!

Sing to the Lord and celebrate with song
    How great is our God!

Great is our Lord with wisdom and love
    How great is our God!

The Lord takes pleasure in the devout
    How great is our God!

Our God gives us peace and love
    How great is our God!

The Lord shows us the way with his words
    How great is our God!

Our God knows us each by name
    How great is our God!

Sing to the Lord with thanksgiving
    How great is our God![24]

My God is an awesome God.

God Is . . .

God is our refuge
God is our strength
God is with us
God is our help

God is merciful
God is trustworthy
God is just
God is faithful

God is our guide
God is our comfort
God will lead us
God will never forsake us

God will hear us
God will rescue us
God delivers us
God is our hope[25]

In the Lord

I trust in the Lord
I find delight in the Lord
My steps are guided in the Lord
I take refuge in the Lord
My salvation is in the Lord[26]

I Love God

I love God with all my heart

I love God with all my soul

I love God with all my spirit

I love God with all my mind

I love God with my whole being

I love God with all my strength

I love God with all my will

I love God with my all and now I live

Above all things I love God!

COMPLEX PRAYERS

What I term/consider Complex Prayers I will try to put into words. It can be one that is very long or at least longer than I normally use. It can be one that I would use in a retreat. It can be a novena used in a 9-day period. It can be an Intercessory or an affirmational prayer.

A Pandemic Prayer for Protection

Heavenly Father, Creator God,
Hear our prayers!

Protect us during this Pandemic.
Watch over and heal your people.

Help those that are healthy and working.
Help those that are sick and recovering.

Help those that are First Responders.
Help those that are Hospital Workers.

Help those at home.
Help those that lead our nation.

May we all increase our love for God and one another.
May we all increase our faith, hope, and love.

Show your mercy for those who have died.
Show us your compassion and love. Amen.

Affirmations on Healing

- † I am being transformed!
- † I have been redeemed and restored with hope through Jesus.
- † I am liberated from bondage and sin by Jesus.
- † I am a child of God.
- † I know that God is good all the time.
- † I am saved because, Jesus paid the price for me.
- † I am a new creation!
- † I have my identity in Christ.
- † I am thankful and abound with gratitude.
- † I am the temple of the Holy Spirit.
- † I treat others with kindness, forgiveness, and compassion.
- † I radiate faith, hope, and love.
- † I am born again!
- † I am filled with love and God's power.
- † I experience God's healing power.
- † I have peace that surpasses all understanding.
- † I reaffirm positive truths with thanks.
- † I make healthy choices with Jesus.
- † I have been renewed physically, mentally, and spiritually.
- † I am full of faith, hope, and love!
- † I am grateful and I worship God.
- † Nothing is impossible for God!
- † I praise and glorify God, the Trinity. Amen.

A Prayer on the Three Values, Unity, Dignity, and Work

O Lord I pray for our Unity
Unity is for the harmony of people in all their diversity. Unity drives away fear, it recognizes the plurality of political views and religious beliefs.

O Lord I pray for our Dignity
Dignity is the mutual respect and solidarity which is possible, only if everyone recognizes the inherent and equal dignity of all.

O Lord I pray for Work
Work should be available for all, so that they can improve their lives. Through the investment of education and health care one can progress to dignified work. Dignified work or job opportunities would offer anyone a better future. Amen.[27]

The miracle is not that we do this work, but that we are happy to do it. St. Mother Teresa of Calcutta

What Isaiah said about Jesus

He was spurned, a man of suffering.
He was stricken, struck down by God.
It was our infirmities and sufferings that He bore.
He was pierced for our offenses.
He was crushed for our sins.

The Lord, Carried the guilt of us all.
He bore retribution for our sin, now we are whole.
By his stripes we were healed.

He was harshly treated.
He was led to the slaughter.
He was silent, not a word from His mouth.
He was oppressed and condemned.
He was taken away.
He was cut off from the land of the living.
He was smitten for the sins of His people.
He had done no wrong.
He spoke no falsehood.
He gave his life as an offering for our sin.

God's will shall be accomplished through Him.
Through His sufferings, my servant shall justify many.
He bore our iniquities.
He surrendered Himself to death.
He bore the sins of many.
He interceded for our offenses.[28]

Franciscan Order

A Franciscan's Prayer Method

Saint Francis of Assisi, from the thirteenth century, has an attitude of openness and willingness to follow the Spirit. This type of prayer is marked by a spirit of being free, unconfined, and allowing the Spirit to move him or her. The person who prays a Franciscan type prayer is committed to do God's will and is not tied down by rules.

The person inclined to pray in this realm is cheerful, light-hearted, optimistic, and they thrive on challenge. Franciscan spirituality is very popular among ordinary men and women. These people are committed to acts of loving service; fraternal love in doing God's will is their main goal.

Franciscan spirituality is very optimistic, and sees the beauty, goodness, and love of God everywhere. In addition, they are led by free-flowing, spontaneous, informal praising, and loving dialog with God. Also, they are very forgiving in their attitude. It is said that Franciscan Prayer makes use of all the five senses.

One important aspect is that Francis Assisi understood that the Incarnation of God, Jesus, is the visible, audible, tangible presence of God; who came down from heaven.

Another aspect of Franciscan Spirituality is their motto "Seize the Day" which follows the teaching of Jesus: Do not be concerned about tomorrow. It will have troubles enough of its own. Sufficient for the day is the trouble thereof. *(Mt 6:34)*

Franciscan Spirituality is interested in the literal sense of the Bible; they are interested in the reality of the Scripture to their lives. Many of the greatest saints, who showed an enormous amount of generosity prayed with this method. They love spontaneous prayer to celebrate the goodness, greatness, and love of God.[29]

Blessing of Saint Francis
(see Common Franciscan Prayers)

May the Lord bless you.

May the Lord keep you.

May the Lord show you mercy.

May the Lord show you peace.

Amen.

Augustinian Order

An Augustinian's Prayer Method

The Augustinian Method of Prayer has been used by the Fathers of the Church throughout the centuries. The key word to help describe this Augustinian Prayer is transposition. Through this transposition process one uses his or her creative imagination to transpose the words of the Scripture to our situation today. One tries to imagine the words of the scripture spoken to him or her today.

Throughout the course of history several writers, preachers, teachers, and ordinary lay people have used this method. This process is aligned with intuition and feeling of the participant. The person using this method has an interest in the current application and with future possibilities. The participant tries to discern the will of God within today's context.

Through the Bible God speaks to us. Through prayer we speak to God. When using this method, we develop a dialog between God and ourself. With meditation we strive toward a personal development of our relationship with God. One personalizes the insights obtained through this process to discern God's will. Being able to understand the discernment of God's Wisdom while applying it to our situation of today. Determining the will of God is the hope of many! When discerning, one needs to be open to the Holy Spirit's prompting and apply the deeper meaning within the word of God.

This dialog between God and oneself can be accomplished by using the four steps of *Lectio Divina*: Read, Meditate, Pray, and Contemplation.

Ask yourself these questions:
What do these words of Scripture that I just read mean to me in my present situation?

– and –

What message is the Lord trying to convey to me in the ancient words of the Bible?[30]

Rest in You
(see St. Augustine of Hippo)

O Lord God,
give us peace,
for you give us all things:
the peace of rest,
Yes, give us rest in you.
Amen.

Thomistic Philosophy

The Thomistic Prayer Method

This method of praying is associated with the name of Saint Thomas Aquinas, because it uses a method of rational thinking. It is also known as a Scholastic Method of praying in orderly, progression of thought. Paying close attention to the process of rational thinking and arriving at the appropriate conclusions.

Most Christians from the seventeenth century to the twentieth century have been using this method. It certainly is used by many who have written about meditation and a rationalistic approach to prayer. To use this method of prayer in preparation of the Sacrament of Reconciliation is an excellent choice.

This is adaptable to men and women who thirst for the truth, knowledge, understanding, and comprehending the word of God. They are like the modern-day scientist, investigating the causes behind the word or other actions. They are very systematical in their approach to the Word of God.

This type of prayer is logical, rational, and contemplative. The Thomistic prayer method earnestly seeks the truth about the subject. One way of accomplishing this is to ask the questions: who, what, where, when, and why.

The method used to pray with this is *Lectio Divina*. This dialog between God and oneself can be accomplished by using the four steps of *Lectio Divina*: Read, Meditate, Pray, and Contemplation.[31]

St. Thomas Aquinas Prayer
(see St. Thomas' Daily Prayer)

O merciful God, grant that I may desire ardently,
search prudently, recognize truly, and bring to perfect
completion whatever is pleasing to You
for the praise and glory of Your name.
Put my life in order, O my God. Amen.

"Grant me, O Lord my God, a mind to know you, a heart to seek you, wisdom to find you, conduct pleasing to you, faithful perseverance in waiting for you, and a hope of finally embracing you. Amen."[75]

St Thomas Aquinas

Ignatian / Jesuit Order

An Ignatian Prayer Method

About a thousand years before the birth of Christ the Israelites prayed in a way that commemorated its history, salvation history, recalling specific events. The Israelites celebrate their Passover Event yearly, commemorating their deliverance from the slavery of Egypt.

Christians have continued the use of this type of prayer; specifically, Saint Ignatius of Loyola, the founder of the Jesuit Orders used this under the title of Spiritual Exercises. When using this type of prayer, the participant projects themselves into the historical happening, becoming a part of the event. The best example of this type of prayer by Christians today is Holy Week; beginning with Palm Sunday, thru Easter Sunday. It commemorates each part of the Passion, Death, and Resurrection of Jesus Christ.

Out of a sense of duty, the participant uses scripture stories to draw their mind and heart into the past. In addition, new insights allow one to advance in their spiritual growth on their journey toward God. This type of prayer allows one to draw practical insights and then progress in their life of faith. The purpose is to try to make the scripture scene become alive and real to the participant. It allows one to commemorate and to internalize the message.

Using the four-step process of the Lectio Divina is common to the use of this type of prayer: Read, Meditate, Pray, and Contemplation.

Saint Ignatius also developed a ten-step process to be used during his Spiritual Exercises.

1. Choose the Topic
2. Prepare the Prayer

3. Put yourself into the Scene
4. Pray for Grace
5. See and Reflect
6. Listen and Reflect
7. Consider and Reflect
8. Draw practical Insights
9. Unite with the Trinity
10. Closing with the "Our Father"[32]

Prayer of St. Ignatius

(see www.providence.org)

Lord, receive all my liberty, my memory, my understanding, my whole will, all that I have and all that I possess. You gave it all to me, Lord; I give it all back to you. Do with it as you will, according to your good pleasure. Amen.

Benedictine Order

Benedictine Prayer Method *(Lectio Divina)*

Benedictine prayer method extends back to the fourth and fifth centuries. It's a traditional Benedictine practice of scriptural reading, meditation and prayer intended to promote communion with God and to increase the knowledge of God's Word. This is using the four-step process of *Lectio Divina*: Read, Meditate, Pray, and Contemplation.

Lectio *(Reading)* – uses the word of God *(or other spiritual readings)*. Writings in the Bible have been inspired by the Holy Spirit; understand that God inspires others also. Some say works of art can also be used. Teaches us a lesson.

Meditatio *(Meditation)* – uses meditation *(thinking/intellect)* to reflect on insights. Personalize the message with how does it pertain to me? Bring to life the meaning of the Word to your daily life.

Oratio *(Prayer)* – uses one's feelings to enter a dialog with God with prayer. your response to an insight obtained and what changes you want to make in your life. Next, incorporate the Word of God into your heart and into your very life.

Contemplatio *(Contemplation)* – uses one's intuition to coalesce the experiences of the first three steps by contemplating the insights obtained. This is a time just to be quiet, to listen to the Holy Spirit within. This fourth step is also referred to as "Resting in the Lord" it is Contemplative Prayer.

We can be assured that our Lectio Divina has been successful and God has truly touched us when we have an increase of the fruit of the Spirit's virtues. As the Word of God proclaims in *Gal 5:22*. We can incorporate these virtues into our life, summarized as: love, joy, peace, patience, kindness, generosity, faithfulness, gentleness, and self-control.[33]

A Prayer to Seek and Find God
(see belmontabbey.org/prayers)

Father, in your goodness
grant me the intellect to comprehend you,
the perception to discern you,
and the reason to appreciate you.

In your kindness
endow me with the diligence to look for you,
the wisdom to discover you,
and the spirit to apprehend you.

In your graciousness
bestow on me a heart to contemplate you,
ears to hear you,
eyes to see you,
and a tongue to speak of you.

In your mercy to confer on me
a conversation pleasing to you,
the patience to wait for you,
and the perseverance to long for you.

Grant me a perfect end, your holy presence.
I ask this in the name of your Son,
Our Lord Jesus Christ. Amen.

Praying the Names of the Triune God

Jesus, Holy Spirit, & God the Father

The next section is a Litany pertaining to the names of Jesus, Holy Spirit, and God. It can be read through to focus one's mind and heart on the Holy Names of Jesus, Holy Spirit, and God. I used it in a retreat setting to help with a deeper spirituality and a deeper holiness. It can be read through by the Retreat Master or used like a responsorial, where the responder repeats the phrase again.

Praying the Names of Jesus

(A Litany of the Names of Jesus)

Jesus is the Author of Salvation
Jesus is the Bread of Life
Jesus is the Cornerstone
Jesus is the Rock
Jesus is the Alpha and the Omega
Jesus is the First and Last
Jesus is the Root and offspring of David
Jesus is the Messiah
Jesus is the Lion of the Tribe of Judah
Jesus is the Anointed One
Jesus is the Deliverer
Jesus is the High Priest
Jesus is the Faithful and True Witness
Jesus is the King of Kings
Jesus is the Lord of Lords
Jesus is the Redeemer
Jesus is the Gate
Jesus is the Mighty God
Jesus is the Second Person of the Trinity

Jesus is the Wonderful Counselor
Jesus is the Good Shepherd
Jesus is the Holy One
Jesus is Immanuel
Jesus is the Judge
Jesus is the Lamb of God
Jesus is the Light of the World
Jesus is the Mediator
Jesus is the Physician
Jesus is the Prince of Peace
Jesus is the Radiance of your Glory
Jesus is the Word of Life
Jesus is the Savior
Jesus is the Way, the Truth, and the Life

"All power in heaven and on earth has been given to me. Go therefore, and make disciples of all nations, baptizing them in the name of the Father, and of the Son, and of the Holy Spirit, teaching them to observe all that I have commanded you. And behold, I am with you always, until the end of the age." *(Mt 28:18b-20)*

Praying the Names of the Holy Spirit
(A Litany of the Names of the Holy Spirit)

Pure Gift of God
Indwelling Presence
Promise of the Father
Life of Jesus
Eternal Praise
Inner Anointing
Reminder of the Mystery
Knower of All Things
Implanted Peacemaker
Magnetic Center
God's Compass
Inner Breath
Hidden Love of God
Implanted Hope
Fire of Life and Love
Sacred Peacemaker
Truth Speaker
Great Bridge Builder
Warmer of Hearts
Flowing Stream
Wind of Change
Descending Dove
Great Compassion
God's Happiness
The Will of God[34]

Come, Holy Spirit and enkindle in me the fire of your love.

Praying the Names of God

(A Litany of the Names of God)

God, Mighty Creator
God Almighty
God Most High
The God Who Sees Me
The Everlasting God
The Eternal God
The Lord Will Provide
The Lord and Master
The Lord Who heals
The Lord My Banner
The Lord is Peace
The Lord of Hosts
The Lord My Rock
The Lord is My Shepherd
The Consuming Fire
The Living God
The Holy One of Israel
The Strong Tower
The Hope of Israel
The Lord, Our Righteousness
My Strength
My Rock
My Fortress
My Dwelling Place
My Refuge
My Shield
My Deliverer
Our King
Our Judge
Our Father[35]

Abba, Abba Father, you are the Potter, we are the clay, the work of your hands.

Praying the Psalms

At a Men's Retreat a couple of years ago we focused on the Psalms. I have presented many times at the Men's Retreat, and have made a litany of all 150 Psalms. I would say the below phrases and then the participants would repeat it again as a response.

1. The law of the Lord is their joy.
2. Happy are those who take refuge in God.
3. You Lord, are my shield.
4. I trust in the Lord.
5. To you I pray, O Lord.
6. Have pity on me Lord, for I am weak.
7. You are the God who saves.
8. My Lord, how awesome is your name.
9. I will praise you Lord, with all my heart.
10. The Lord is King forever.
11. The Lord is just and loves just deeds.
12. Lord, protect us always.
13. O God, give light to my eyes.
14. The Lord restores.
15. Never be shaken.
16. You will show me the path to life.
17. Lord, listen to my prayer.
18. I love you Lord.
19. The heavens declare the glory of God.
20. May God send help.
21. There's joy in your presence.
22. I will proclaim your name.
23. The Lord is my shepherd.
24. Seek the face of God.
25. I lift up my soul.
26. In the Lord I trust.

27. The Lord is my light and my salvation.
28. The Lord is my strength and my shield.
29. Bow down before the Lord.
30. Lord always be my helper.
31. Let me never be put to shame.
32. I confess my faults to the Lord.
33. By the Lord's Word, the heavens were made.
34. I will bless the Lord at all times.
35. Lord please say, 'I Am your salvation.'
36. How precious is your love, O God!
37. Trust in the Lord and do good.
38. Forsake me not, O Lord.
39. You are my only hope.
40. To do your will is my delight.
41. Lord have mercy on me.
42. My soul longs for you, O God.
43. God, defend me.
44. You are my King and my God.
45. Nations shall praise you forever.
46. God is my refuge and my strength.
47. The Lord, the Most High, inspires.
48. Great is the Lord.
49. God will redeem my life.
50. I offer praise as my sacrifice to God.
51. Have mercy on me, God.
52. I will praise you always.
53. I will seek God, rejoice and be glad.
54. O God hear my prayer.
55. The Lord will save me.
56. In you I trust, I do not fear.
57. I call to God Most High.
58. The just shall rejoice.
59. Rescue me from my enemies.

60. Help me God.
61. Hear my cry, O God.
62. My soul rests in God alone.
63. O God, I long for you.
64. I take refuge in the Lord.
65. May we be filled with goodness.
66. Shout joyfully to God.
67. May God's face shine upon us.
68. God is our salvation.
69. I pray to you Lord.
70. Graciously rescue me God.
71. You are my rock and my hope.
72. May Gods name be blessed forever.
73. Lord God you are my refuge.
74. You God are my King.
75. We thank you God.
76. You are an awesome God.
77. Your way O God, is Holy.
78. Trust in God.
79. Pardon our sins.
80. God save us and restore us.
81. Sing joyfully to the Lord.
82. Rescue the lowly and poor.
83. Lord the Most High.
84. Happy are those who find refuge in you.
85. O Lord, I will listen to your Word.
86. Teach me your way, O Lord.
87. Within you is my true home.
88. I cry out to you, O Lord.
89. Love is established forever.
90. May we gain wisdom of heart.
91. My God in whom I trust.
92. I proclaim your love.

93. Holiness belongs to your house, Lord.
94. Happy are those you guide.
95. Hear his voice.
96. Sing to the Lord.
97. The Lord is King.
98. Shout with joy.
99. Exalt the Lord, our God.
100. Love endures forever.
101. I act with integrity.
102. Lord, hear my prayer.
103. Bless the Lord, my soul.
104. The Lord endures forever.
105. Give thanks to the Lord.
106. Happy are those who do right.
107. God is our Savior.
108. Awaken my soul.
109. Save me in your kindness.
110. I begotten you, says the Lord.
111. I praise the Lord with all my heart.
112. Our hearts are tranquil, without fear.
113. Praise, you servants of the Lord.
114. The God of Jacob.
115. Our God in heaven.
116. I love the Lord.
117. The Lord is faithful forever.
118. Give thanks to the Lord.
119. Walk by the teaching of the Lord.
120. Lord, deliver me.
121. The Lord is my guardian.
122. May those who love You prosper!
123. To You I raise my eyes.
124. Our help is in the name of the Lord.
125. Trust in the Lord.

126. The Lord has done great things.
127. The Lord builds the house.
128. Walk in the ways of God.
129. May the blessings of the Lord be upon us.
130. With the Lord is kindness.
131. I have hope in the Lord.
132. Let us worship God.
133. The Lord is life everlasting.
134. Come, bless the Lord.
135. Praise the Lord; the Lord is good!
136. God's love endures forever.
137. We sing a song of hope.
138. You strengthened my spirit, O Lord.
139. Lord, you know me, you understand me.
140. Deliver me Lord, from the wicked.
141. Lord, I call on you.
142. You are my refuge.
143. Lord, hear my prayer.
144. Lord, you are my shield, in whom I trust.
145. My God and King.
146. The Lord protects.
147. Sing to the Lord with thanksgiving.
148. Praise the Lord's name.
149. Let the faithful rejoice.
150. Give praise to the Lord our God!

Lord, hear my prayer.

The Sermon on the Mount *(The Beatitudes)*

When he saw the crowds, he went up the mountain, and after he had sat down, his disciples came to him. He began to teach them, saying:

- † Blessed are the poor in spirit, for theirs is the kingdom of heaven.
- † Blessed are they who mourn, for they will be comforted.
- † Blessed are the meek, for they will inherit the land.
- † Blessed are they who hunger and thirst for righteousness, for they will be satisfied.
- † Blessed are the merciful, for they will be shown mercy.
- † Blessed are the clean of heart, for they will see God.
- † Blessed are the peacemakers, for they will be called children of God.
- † Blessed are they who are persecuted for the sake of righteousness, for theirs is the kingdom of heaven.
- † Blessed are you when they insult you and persecute you and utter every kind of evil against you [falsely] because of me.
- † Rejoice and be glad, for your reward will be great in heaven. Thus, they persecuted the prophets who were before you.[36]

The way our life has been transformed by the Beatitudes, our words, thoughts & deeds show that we are true followers of Christ. We are therefore, Blessed, Happy, and Holy with our Lord Jesus.[37]

MONTHLY INTERCESSORY PRAYER

What is intercessory prayer?

Intercessory prayer is the act of praying on behalf of others. It was prevalent in the Old Testament, in the cases of Abraham, Moses, David, Samuel, Elijah, Jeremiah, Ezekiel, and Daniel. Christ is pictured in the New Testament as the ultimate intercessor, and because of this, all Christian prayer becomes an intercession since it is offered to God through Christ. Jesus closed the gap between us and God when he died on the cross. Jesus can now intercede in prayer on behalf of believers asking God to grant their requests according to his will.

The Holy Spirit Intercedes with Our Prayers

(Scripture Rom 8:25-27) If we hope for what we do not see, we wait with endurance. In the same way, the Spirit too comes to the aid of our weakness; for we do not know how to pray as we ought, but the Spirit itself intercedes with inexpressible groanings. And the one who searches hearts knows what is the intention of the Spirit, because it intercedes for the holy ones according to God's will.[38]

We, though many, are one body in Christ and individually parts of one another. *(Rom 12:5)*

January Intercessory Prayer

Pray for Christian Unity

Heavenly Father, we pray for the Christians throughout our local community, our country, and the world to become unified. We need to put away our differences and think about our similarities. We need to put away our anger and show our love toward one another. We need to put away our perspective of us versus them.

Father grant us love, patience, and kindness. We need to strive for forgiveness and understanding. We all have free will and God allows us to use that free will. The thousands of denominations and churches proves our need for unity. Let us have faith in Jesus, who is the way, the truth, and the life *(Jn 14:6)*. Let us have hope that we can become a citizen of heaven if Jesus is our Lord. We need to aspire to follow the narrow path of love and righteousness. Let us be an example to others with our love of God and one another. As the scripture indicates, they'll know we are Christians by our love. Amen.

Jan. 18-25, A Week of Prayer for Christian Unity
Scriptures: ... they may all become One ... *(Jn 17:21)*
This is how all will know that you are my disciples,
if you have love for one another. *(Jn 13:36)*

February Intercessory Prayer

Forgiveness

Heavenly Father, we have all been slighted. We have all held anger or a grudge against another. We have all been perturbed because of someone's actions against us. These infractions against our person cause us to shun that person. These infractions against us cause internal injury. These infractions against us wage a war within if allowed to fester and make us bitter.

Let us overcome any hard feelings toward another. Let us overcome any anger toward another. Let us overcome any animosity toward another. We know that these feelings can last for years. We know that these feeling of ours don't normally hurt the other person, but hurt us mentally, emotionally, and physically. Therefore, let us give it up to you Lord. Help us show forgiveness and love! Amen.

Days to Remember: Marriage Day, Valentine's Day
Scripture: Forgive and you will be forgiven. *(Lk 6:37b)*
But if you do not forgive others, neither will your Father forgive your transgressions. *(Mt 6:15a)*

Father, forgive them, they know not what they do. *(Lk 23:34a)*

March Intercessory Prayer

A Prayer for Those in Need

Heavenly Father,
I pray for my family, the church, and the world.
I pray for the lost, wounded, and abandoned.
I pray for the poor, homeless, and destitute.
I pray for the needy, neglected, and unemployed.
I pray for the weak in mind, body, and spirit.
I pray for the oppressed, abused, and persecuted.
I pray for the helpless, intimidated, and manipulated.
I pray for those in trouble, in despair, and suffering.
I pray for those without food, clothing, or shelter.
I pray for those lonely, without loved ones, and are isolated.
I pray for those who are mourning, in pain, and in distress.
I pray for those who are injured, sick, and dying.
I pray for those who are weak, defenseless, and enslaved.
I pray for those facing discrimination, poverty, and violence.
I pray for those from broken homes, divorced, and separated.
I pray for all the unborn, the babies, and the innocent children.
Amen.

Days to Remember: Ash Wednesday & St. Patrick's Day
Scriptures: Pray for one another *(Jas 5:16)* and Blessed are you who are poor for the kingdom of God is yours. *(Lk 6:20)*

April Intercessory Prayer

A Grateful heart

Heavenly Father,

We pray that you help bring a loving, compassionate, and grateful heart to those throughout the United States and throughout the World. Please change the hardened heart of those that do not show love and appreciation to others. Please change the heart of those who do not show love and compassion to others. Please change the heart of those who do not show love and generosity to others. Heavenly Father bring about your mercy and grace to help people change. Amen.

- † I praise your holy name Lord.
- † I exalt you over all others Lord.
- † I thank you with all my heart Lord.
- † Lord you strengthen my spirit.
- † Lord I love to hear your holy word.
- † Lord how great is your glory.
- † The Lord cares for the lowly.
- † The Lord saves me and loves me.
- † The Lord is with me forever and ever. Amen.

Days to Remember: Palm Sunday, Good Friday, Easter, and Earth Day
Scripture: Psalm 138 "Hymn of a Grateful heart."

May Intercessory Prayer

Precious to The Lord

Heavenly Father,

Let us help build up the body of Christ and consider all Christians are one in spirit. Let us pray for those in the body of Christ. Let us all exhibit the virtues that should be shown by those in the body of Christ. God bless us and the body of Christ with your grace. your word says, "We are precious to the Lord!" Amen.

- † We are precious to the Lord, when we show love.
- † We are precious to the Lord, when we are patient.
- † We are precious to the Lord, when we show kindness.
- † We are precious to the Lord, when we show forgiveness.
- † We are precious to the Lord, when we are compassionate.
- † We are precious to the Lord, when we are joyful.
- † We are precious to the Lord, when we are at peace.
- † We are precious to the Lord, when we are humble.

Days to Remember: A National Day of Prayer and Mother's Day Memorial Day and Ascension of Jesus
Scripture: the LORD regards my life as precious (*1 Sam 26:24*)

June Intercessory Prayer

Pray for Our Country

Heavenly Father,

Let us honor America this month; God bless our country! Each day it seems as if our country is going down a dark path. It seems that people are distrustful of one another. It seems that people are showing signs of hatred and anger. It seems that people are more divided than ever.

God please soften people's hearts. Help us to lead others to your holy light. Help us lead others down the path of light with love, joy, and peace. Help us to lead others to your joy.

- † Dispel the darkness with light.
- † Reduce fear with trust.
- † Decrease gloom with joy.
- † Abandon division with unity.
- † Eliminate hate with love. Amen.

Days to Remember: Honor America, Pentecost, Flag Day, Father's Day, and Corpus Christi
Scripture: When you pray, go to your inner room, close the door, and pray to your Father in secret. And your Father who sees in secret will repay you. *(Mt 6:6)*

July Intercessory Prayer

A Prayer for Children and Grandchildren

Heavenly Father,

Thank you for blessing me with children and grandchildren.
Father I love my children and grandchildren with all my heart.

Father give them your mercy and grace.
Father give them a great abundance of faith, hope, and love.

Father give them your protection from the challenges of life.
Father give them your insight, understanding, and wisdom.

Father may they have health, happiness, and long life.
Father may they have the courage to follow their dreams.

Father may they never forget that they are always loved by me.
Father may they always know your love as I have. Amen.[39]

Days to Remember: Independence Day and Parents Day
Scripture: Jesus said, "Let the children come to me, and do not prevent them; for the kingdom of heaven belongs to such as these." *(Mt 19:14)*

Pray for your children. *(Wis 13:17)*

August Intercessory Prayer

Endure Testing

Heavenly Father,

We pray for all those being tested. We are all tested each day by the Evil One, the Devil Satan. We all have been tested through being hurt, being hungry, and being tired. Help us to endure the testing of this world and help us with your consolation. We ask for you to give us our daily bread.

The Bible tells us that Jesus prayed to overcome the struggles of life. The Holy Spirit will help us and teach us how to pray. We pray to endure the challenges of life. We also pray for ourselves, our loved ones, and our friends. We pray for our community, our country, and our world. Father show us the path to truth and life! Father give us your peace! Lord, all we want, is to rest in you. Amen.

Days to Remember: Transfiguration of the Lord and Assumption of the Blessed Virgin Mary
Scriptures: The Lord, your God is testing you.
(Deut 13:4)

Know that the testing of your faith produces perseverance. *(Jas 1:3b)*

September Intercessory Prayer

A Prayer for Peace

Almighty Father,

I know for you nothing is impossible. I ask for peace! I want the joy and happiness you have for anyone who follows you. I want the joy and happiness you have for myself and my family. I know there is nothing in this world that can give me true joy, happiness, and peace. You are my joy and my happiness. I rest in you.

I pray for peace in our world, our country, and our universal church. Help all people understand one another and live together in peace & harmony. Bring peace to all of us Lord God, we need our hearts to rest in you. Amen.

Days to Remember: Labor Day and Grandparents Day
Patriot Day: A National Day of Prayer and Remembrance – September 11 (9/11).

Scripture: When you pray, go to your inner room, close the door, and pray to your Father in secret. And your Father who sees in secret will repay you. *(Mt 6:6)*

October Intercessory Prayer

Saving Others

Heavenly Father,

I pray for all those who do not know you, your Son, or the Holy Spirit. Please help us pass-on the Good News in our daily interactions. Please help us through our prayers to intercede for those who do not know or believe in the Trinity. Please help us on our mission to build up the Body of Christ.

Heavenly Father, we know there are those who need to learn about your Son Jesus Christ; we commit to that mission with those we meet. There are also those who deny the truth; Father show them mercy, soften their hearts, and lead them to the truth.

Heavenly Father, we know the Scripture 'For God so loved the world that he gave his only begotten Son' *(Jn 3:16)*. Let us all pray for others, and witness to others, the gospel message. Your salvation is available to those who love you, help us have faith in Jesus Christ, and believe he is the Son of God. This I pray to God the Father, through the Lord Jesus, with the Holy Spirit, and my Guardian Angel. Amen.

Days to Remember: Guardian Angels & Columbus Day
Scripture: You may be an instrument of salvation. *(Acts 13:47)*

November Intercessory Prayer

A Change of Heart

At times we have a heart of stone. We might even have anger and hatred in our heart. We might even hold grudges, with un-forgiveness in our heart. We might even have impatience in our heart. We need to change! We need to love one another.

Heavenly Father help us to love one another. Please grant us:

- † A heart of love.
- † A heart of patience.
- † A heart of humility.
- † A heart of kindness.
- † A heart of forgiveness.
- † A heart of compassion.
- † A heart of peace.

Thank you, heavenly Father, for your grace. Amen.

Days to Remember: All Saints' Day, Veterans Day and Thanksgiving
Scripture: Have a change of heart. *(Bar 2:30)*

December Intercessory Prayer

A Family Prayer

Heavenly Father,

I come to you in prayer with a humble heart. Father I ask for your forgiveness for any sins I have committed. Father I pray for your mercy and grace for myself, my family, and my friends. I pray that we all have good health, happiness, and a long life. May we be infused with faith, hope, and love. May we have peace and joy in life. May we all be transformed; may we all develop a deep spirituality, a deep conversion, a deep holiness toward the Father, Son and Holy Spirit.

Father give us grace to endure the challenges of life. Father at the end, allow me to say: Into your hands I commend my spirit. Father at the end may you say: Well done good and faithful servant. Father at the end allow me to enter into heaven with you forever and ever. I pray this to you God the Father, through Jesus Christ, with the Holy Spirit; with Mary the Mother of God, my Guardian Angel, and in Communion with all the Angels and Saints. To you Almighty Father be the glory forever and ever. Amen.

Days to Remember: Immaculate Conception of the Blessed Virgin Mary, Christmas, and New Year's Eve

Scripture: Let us do good to all, but especially to those who belong to the family of the faith. *(Gal 6:10)*

PRAYERS FROM SAINTS

The prayers from the saints will include a few prayers directly from the Bible. Some of these will be short and concise; some will be longer and more complex.

Quotes from Saints and Scripture

- † For God so loved the world that he gave his only Son, so that everyone who believes in him might not perish but might have eternal life.[40]
- † Come be My Light.[41]
- † Speak, Lord, for your servant is listening.[42]
- † Lord purify my mind and heart.[43]
- † Be an Instrument of Peace.[44]
- † The Lord God is my help; therefore, I am not disgraced.[45]
- † All things work for good for those who love God.[46]
- † Here I am Lord.[47]
- † Here I am, send me![48]
- † Jesus, I trust in you.[49]
- † You have the words of eternal life.
- † Well done, my good and faithful servant.[50]
- † God loves each of us as if there were only one of us.[51]
- † I give you a new commandment; love one another.[52]

- † Love is the beauty of the soul.[53]
- † Preach the Gospel at all times and when necessary use words.[54]
- † I am not afraid; I was born to do this.[55]
- † Let nothing disturb you, let nothing frighten you, all things are passing away, God never changes.[56]
- † He who trusts himself is lost. He who trusts in God can do all things.[57]
- † The one who sent me is with me.[58]
- † The dead that hear the voice of the Son of God, and those who hear will live.[59]
- † The Lord comforts his people.[60]
- † Jesus said, "I am with you always, until the end of age."[61]
- † O Lord, my God, in you I take refuge.[62]
- † For the sake of His sorrowful Passion, have mercy on us and on the whole world.[63]
- † The Lord bless you and keep you! The Lord let his face shine upon you and be gracious to you! The Lord look upon you kindly and give you peace![64]
- † Lord, make me an instrument of your peace, where there is hatred, let me sow love; where there is injury, pardon; where there is doubt, faith; where there is despair, hope; where there is darkness, light; and where there is sadness, joy.[65]
- † Peter said, "Repent and be baptized, every one of you, in the name of Jesus Christ for the forgiveness of your sins; and you will receive the gift of the Holy Spirit. For the promise is made to you and to your children and to all those far off, whomever the Lord our God will call."[66]
- † Awaken and enlighten us, my Lord, that we might know and love the blessings which you ever propose to us, and that we might understand that You have moved to bestow favors on us and have remembered us. Amen.[67]
- † We can do no great things, only small things with great love.[68]

Prayer for Protection

The light of Christ surrounds me.
The love of Christ enfolds me.
The power of Christ protects me.
The presence of Christ watches over me. Amen.[69]

Act of Petition

Give me yourself, O my God, give yourself to me. Behold I love you, and if my love is too weak a thing, grant me to love you more strongly. I cannot measure my love to know how much it falls short of being sufficient, but let my soul hasten to your embrace and never be turned away until it is hidden in the secret shelter of your presence. This only do I know, that it is not good for me when you are not with me, when you are only outside me. I want you in my very self. All the plenty in the world which is not my God is utter want. Amen.[70]

Act of Offering

Jesus, you have given yourself to me, Now let me give myself to you; I give you my body, that it may be chaste and pure. I give you my soul, that it may always love you. I give you every thought, word, and deed of my life, and I offer all for your honor and glory. Amen.[71]

Teach me to be Generous

Lord, teach me to be generous; to serve you as you deserve; to give and not to count the cost, to fight and not to heed the wounds, to toil and not to seek for rest, to labor and not to look for any reward, save that of knowing that I do your holy will. Amen.[72]

Prayer of Love

O love eternal, my soul needs and chooses you eternally! Ah, come Holy Spirit, and inflame our hearts with your love! To love - or to die! To die - and to love! To die to all other love in order to live in Jesus' love, so that we may not die eternally. But that we may live in your eternal love, O Savior of our souls, we eternally sing, "Live, Jesus! Jesus, I love! Live, Jesus, whom I love! Jesus, I love, Jesus who lives and reigns forever and ever. Amen.[73]

Grant to Me ...

Grant me, O Lord my God, a mind to know you, a heart to seek you, wisdom to find you, conduct pleasing to you, faithful perseverance in waiting for you, and a hope of finally embracing you. Amen.[74]

I pray for those who will believe in me, so that they may all be one, as you, Father, are in me and I in you. *(see Jn 17:20-21a)*

Prayer to Love God

I love you, O my God, and my only desire is to love you until the last breath of my life. I love you, O my infinitely lovable God, and I would rather die loving you than live without loving you. I love you, Lord and the only grace I ask is to love you eternally... My God, if my tongue cannot say in every moment that I love you, I want my heart to repeat it to you as often as I draw breath. Amen.[75]

A Student's Prayer *(Modified)*

God our creator and the true source of light and wisdom. Pour forth your brilliance upon my intellect, dissipate all darkness and sin within me. Grant me ease of learning, a mind to understand, and a retentive memory. Grant me your wisdom and the grace to express myself with your love. I ask through Jesus Christ and the Holy Spirit. Amen.[76]

Prayer for Discipleship

Lord Jesus Christ, truth and life,

I understand that humility, patience and love are necessary to be a disciple of yours. I seek you, Father, Son, and Holy Spirit; the Trinity of the Universe. I exercise reason and love with all my soul. I found contentment with God and I rest in you. 'In God Alone!' Amen.[77]

Who Can Be Against Us?

If God is for us, who can be against us?[78]

Peace Prayer

Lord, make me an instrument of your peace: where there is hatred, let me sow love; where there is injury, pardon; where there is doubt, faith; where there is despair, hope; where there is darkness, light; and where there is sadness, joy.

Grant that I may not so much seek to be consoled as to console, to be understood as to understand, to be loved as to love. For it is in giving that we receive, it is in pardoning that we are pardoned, and it is in dying that we are born to eternal life. Amen.[79]

The Simple Path

- † →SILENCE
- † The fruit of silence is
- † PRAYER
- † The fruit of prayer is
- † →FAITH
- † The fruit of faith is
- † →LOVE
- † The fruit of love is
- † →SERVICE
- † The fruit of service is
- † →PEACE[41]

Let there be peace on Earth and let it begin with me.

CHAPLAIN PRAYERS

A Chaplain meets people where they are spiritually. To pray for and help people; to be all inclusive of all religions & faiths is important to a Chaplain's mindset. Chaplains understand this mercy of God to heal people physically, emotionally, and spiritually. Therefore, the Chaplain's mindset includes healing people at their level of belief, to best help them. God reveals himself to each of us at our own pace. This revelation is different for each person and each religion. *(as an example, there are at least 40,000 different Christian faiths, although similar, they have their own beliefs that separate them from each other).*

Below are a number of prayers I have researched to help me in this endeavor. I feel that anyone as a Chaplain could benefit from the use of these prayers.

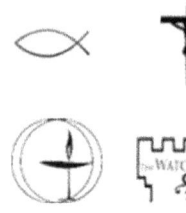

<u>As a Hospital Chaplain</u>

We help people to find peace and tranquility. To communicate with their Creator. We help them find their center the best way we can with a listening ear; and we help them with consolation and peace.

10a) CHRISTIAN PRAYERS

Preparation in Praying
"Lord purify my mind and heart,
Be an Instrument of Peace,
Be his Light, Show Love Always." Amen.

Prayer for the Dead
Our Creator God, in your wisdom you have called your servant *(name(s))* out of this world. Welcome *(him, her, or them)* into your presence, so *(name(s))* may enjoy eternal light and peace with you forever and ever. In Jesus Christ' name we pray. Amen.[80]

Sickness that May Lead to Death
Heavenly Father, I know that my Redeemer lives, and on the final day of my life, his voice shall call to me to rise again. I cherish this hope in my heart. In this hope I will behold my Savior and my Lord. In this hope I will live with God forever and ever. Amen.[81]

The Eight Second Prayer
"Lord I love you and I need you, come into my heart and bless me, my family, my home, and my friends, in Jesus' name." Amen.[82]

Lord help Me

Lord help me purify my mind.
Lord help me purify my heart.
Lord help me be an instrument of peace.
Lord help me be the light of Christ.
Lord help me be an example of your love.
Lord help me show love always. Amen.

Trust in God

Your trust is from God
    Trust in the Lord
Your strength is from God
    Trust in the Lord
Your heart is from God
    Trust in the Lord
Your hope is from God
    Trust in the Lord
Your testing is from God
    Trust in the Lord
Your deeds are from God
    Trust in the Lord
Your reward is from God
    Trust in the Lord[83]

Jesus Our Savior

You are my rock,
You are my fortress,
    Lord Jesus.
Give me mercy,
Give me peace,
    Lord Jesus.
I rejoice in your grace,
I rejoice in your love,
    Lord Jesus.
Through your hands I am saved,
Into your hands I commend my Spirit,
    Lord Jesus. Amen.[84]

Jesus is The Lord

The Lord Jesus Christ is the redeemer
The Lord was there at the beginning
The Lord is the shepherd
The Lord leads you in the path of righteousness
The Lord will give you goodness and kindness
The Lord will give you love and forgiveness
The Lord will give you mercy and grace
And you will dwell in the Lord's house forever[85]

Trust in the Lord

I trust in the Lord
I find delight in the Lord
My steps are guided by the Lord
I take refuge in the Lord
My salvation is in the Lord[86]

His Love Endures Forever

Give thanks to the Lord.
His love endures forever.
The Lord our God is good.
I call out to the Lord in distress.
The Lord our God answers prayers.
The Lord frees me from sinfulness.
I have the Lord at my side.
I have the Lord; I do not fear.
The Lord our God is my helper.
I take refuge in the Lord.
Give thanks to the Lord. Amen.[87]

Prayer for a Medical Procedure

Father God, I am here today with *(name)* for a medical procedure. Please help the doctors who care for *(name)*; help them to be successful. Please help *(name)* to endure it without much pain. Please help heal *(name)* physically, emotionally, and spiritually. Through Jesus Christ's name I pray. Amen.

Love God with all your heart

Love God with all your heart, with all your soul,
and with all your mind.[88]
Love God with all your heart, with all your soul,
and with all your will and might.
Love God with all your heart, with all your soul,
and with all your being and strength.[89]
Love God with all your heart, with all your soul,
so that you may live.[90]
Love and serve the Lord.[91]

Child's Prayer for Protection

God in heaven hear my prayer,
keep me in thy loving care.
Be my guide in all I do,
Bless all those who love me too.
Amen.

God, if you're there come and rescue me !

Prayer for Comfort in Loss

Dear Lord,

Please help me in this time of loss and overwhelming grief. I don't understand why my life is filled with this pain and heartache. But I turn my eyes to you Lord, as I seek to find the strength and trust in your faithfulness. I surrender myself entirely to you O Lord with hope.

My heart is crushed, but I know that you will not abandon me forever. Please show me your compassion, Lord. Help me through the pain. Teach me what is necessary to interior peace.

I believe this promise in your Word, that sends me fresh mercy each day. Though I can't see past today, I trust your great love will never fail me. In this love, I feel comfort and hope in the future. Please help me to find the path of peace, patience, and humility. Amen.

Coping with Fear

Dear Lord,

My fear has trapped and consumed me. But I am tired of living under the weight of my fears. Your Word reassures me of your presence and confirms that you are able to deliver me from my troubles. Please give me your love and your power to replace these fears. Your perfect love casts out my fear. I thank you for promising to give me the peace that only you can give. I receive that peace now as I ask you to still my troubled heart. Because you are with me, I don't have to be afraid. Amen.

Dealing with Stress and Anxiety

Dear Lord,

I need you now because I am full of stress and anxiety. Reading your Word brings comfort, as I ask you to come and take my heavy burdens. I take each burden, one by one, and lay them at your feet.

Please carry them. Replace them with your yoke, for it is meek and humble of heart. For your yoke is easy, and my burden light. I receive your gift of peace of mind and heart. Thank you, that I lie down tonight in peace and sleep. I know that you, Lord, will keep me safe. I am not afraid because you are always with me. Please keep me in your perfect peace.

Amen.[92]

> O Lord, grant me the grace to love you in
> every circumstance, whether I suffer or rejoice.
> I humbly ask this grace of you, Lord Jesus, for your
> greater glory and my eternal salvation. Amen.

10b) CATHOLIC PRAYERS

The Main Essentials of What Prayer is
By Supreme Chaplain Bishop William E. Lori. (Paraphrased)

Prayer is:

Our love for God above all things is rooted in the living Word of God, guided by the Holy Spirit, and taught by the Holy Spirit. We give adoration to our Heavenly Father, humbly acknowledging that we are created by God. In our prayer petitions we ask God for our material needs, and our spiritual needs. We pray for forgiveness of our sins, to grow in Christ likeness, and for His Kingdom to come. We pray for Intercessions for our family and friends. Pray for those who persecute us. Give thanks to God while loving and praising Him. Stay centered on Christ, acknowledging God for our salvation, through Christ our Lord, with the Holy Spirit, to God the Father.[93]

Also, prayer is found in many different forms: adoration, intercession, thanksgiving and praise to name a few. We should include God as prayer in all that we do, and include him in all conversations unceasingly for he is with us always. Additionally, share our faith and God's love with our family, extended family, friends, and all we encounter.

Remember: Mary, 'Called Blessed by all generations,' with her maternal love, leads us to Jesus Christ. We invoke her intercessions through the rosary. We look to the various saints throughout history as examples of how to pray. Saints intercede for us in heaven, with the glory of Christ.

Sign of the Cross

In the name of the Father, and of the Son, and of the Holy Spirit. Amen.

Our Father

Our Father who art in heaven, Hallowed be thy name; thy kingdom come, thy will be done on earth as it is in heaven. Give us this day our daily bread, and forgive us our trespasses, as we forgive those who trespass against us; and lead us not into temptation but deliver us from evil. Amen.

Grace Before Meals

Bless us O Lord and these thy gifts, which we are about to receive from thy bounty, through Christ our Lord. Amen.

Jesus Prayer

Lord Jesus Christ, Son of the living God,
have mercy on me, a sinner. Amen.

Let all mortal flesh keep silence,
and with fear and trembling stand.

Hail Mary

Hail, Mary, full of grace, the Lord is with thee. Blessed art thou among women and blessed is the fruit of thy womb, Jesus. Holy Mary, Mother of God, pray for us sinners, now and at the hour of our death. Amen.

Glory Be

Glory be to the Father and to the Son and to the Holy Spirit. As it was in the beginning, is now, and ever shall be, world without end. Amen.

Prayer to St. Michael

Saint Michael, the Archangel, defend us in battle, be our defense against the wickedness and snares of the devil. May God rebuke him, we humbly pray; and do thou, O Prince of the heavenly host, by the power of God, thrust into Hell Satan and the other evil spirits who prowl about the world for the ruin of souls. Amen.

Act of Contrition

O my God, I am heartily sorry for having offended you. I detest all my sins because of your just punishments. But most of all because they offend you, my God, who are all good and deserving of all my love. I firmly resolve, with the help of your grace to sin no more and to avoid the near occasions of sin. Amen.

Nicene Creed

I believe in one God, the Father almighty, maker of heaven and earth, of all things visible and invisible.

I believe in one Lord Jesus Christ, the Only Begotten Son of God, born of the Father before all ages. God from God, Light from Light, true God from true God, begotten, not made, consubstantial with the Father; through him all things were made. For us men and for our salvation he came down from heaven, and by the Holy Spirit was incarnate of the Virgin Mary, and became man. For our sake he was crucified under Pontius Pilate, he suffered death and was buried, and rose again on the third day in accordance with the Scriptures. He ascended into heaven and is seated at the right hand of the Father. He will come again in glory to judge the living and the dead and his kingdom will have no end. I believe in the Holy Spirit, the Lord, the giver of life, who proceeds from the Father and the Son, who with the Father and the Son is adored and glorified, who has spoken through the prophets. I believe in one, holy, catholic and apostolic Church. I confess one Baptism for the forgiveness of sins and I look forward to the resurrection of the dead and the life of the world to come. Amen.

Act of Contrition *(Catholic UK ver.)*

O my God, because you are so good, I am very sorry that I have sinned against you. With the help of your grace I will try not to sin again. Amen

Soul of Christ *(Anima Christi)*

Soul of Christ, sanctify me;
Body of Christ, save me;
Blood of Christ, inebriate me;
Water from the side of Christ, wash me;
Passion of Christ, strengthen me;
O good Jesus, hear me;
Within thy wounds, hide me;
Permit me not to be separated from Thee;
From the wicked foe defend me;
At the hour of my death call me;
And bid me come to Thee;
That with thy saints I may praise Thee;
For ever and ever. Amen.[94]

> The Holy Spirit was incarnate of the
> Virgin Mary, and became man.

Act of Faith (extended)

O my God, I firmly believe that you are one God in three divine Persons, Father, Son, and Holy Spirit.

I believe that your divine Son became man and died for our sins and that he will come to judge the living and the dead. I believe these and all the truths which the Holy Catholic Church teaches because you have revealed them who are eternal truth and wisdom, who can neither deceive nor be deceived. In this faith I intend to live and die. Amen.[95]

Act of Hope

O Lord God, I hope by your grace for the pardon of all my sins and after life here to gain eternal happiness because you have promised it who are infinitely powerful, faithful, kind, and merciful. In this hope I intend to live and die. Amen.[95]

Act of Love

O Lord God, I love you above all things and I love my neighbor for your sake because you are the highest, infinite, and perfect good, worthy of all my love. In this love I intend to live and die. Amen.[95]

> O Lord fill me with Faith, Hope, and Charity. Fill me with your love so that I can be all of this and do your will.

Offering of Self *(paraphrased)*

Take, Lord, and receive all my liberty, my memory, my intellect, and all my will, all that I have and possess. Thou gravest it to me; to Thee, Lord, I return it. All is Thine, dispose of it wholly according to Thy Will. Give me Thy love and grace, for this is enough for me. Amen.[96]

Prayer Before Working

We beseech you, O Lord, to direct our actions by your holy inspirations, and carry them on by your gracious assistance, that every prayer and work of ours may begin always from you, and through you be happily ended. Amen.[97]

Ablaze with the Fire of your Spirit

O Lord, you have mercy on all, take away from me my sins, and mercifully set me ablaze with the fire of your Holy Spirit. Take away from me the heart of stone, and give me a human heart, a heart to love and adore you, a heart to delight in you, to follow and enjoy you. Amen.[98]

Prayer to St. Michael the Archangel

St. Michael the Archangel, defend us in battle, be our protection against the wickedness and snares of the Devil. May God rebuke him, we humbly pray. And do thou, O Prince of the heavenly Host, by the Power of God, thrust into hell Satan and all evil spirits who wander the earth seeking the ruin of souls. Amen.[99]

Prayer to One's Guardian Angel

Angel of God, my guardian dear, to whom God's love commits me here, ever this day be at my side, to light and guard, to rule, and guide. Amen.

Act of Contrition

I confess to almighty God, and To you, my brothers and sisters, that I have sinned through my own fault, my thoughts, and in my words, in what I have done, and in what I have failed to do; and I ask blessed Mary, ever virgin, all the angels and saints, and you my brothers and sisters, to pray for me to the Lord our God. May almighty God have mercy on us, forgive us our sins, and bring us to everlasting life. Amen.[100]

O Lord, make my heart contrite and humble. You alone can work this miracle. Grant me the pardon that I humbly beg of you. Amen.

Universal Prayer

(Composed by Pope Clement XI and here inserted as a resume' of all the things necessary for eternal salvation. This prayer contains the four books of The Imitation of Christ.)

I believe, O Lord, strengthen my faith; I hope, may I hope with greater certainty; I love, may I love with greater ardor; I am sorry, may I have greater sorrow.

I adore You as the Author of my being; I desire You as my end; I praise You as my perpetual benefactor; I invoke You as my sovereign protector.

Direct me by Your wisdom, restrain me with Your justice; comfort me with Your clemency; protect me with Your power.

I consecrate to You my thoughts, that I may think of You; my words, that I may speak of You; my actions, that they may be according to Your will; my sufferings, for Your greater. glory.

I want what You want, because You want it, as You want it, until You want it.

I beg You to illuminate my intellect, to inflame my will, to purify my body and sanctify my soul.

May I shed tears for my past sins, repulse future temptations, correct my bad inclinations, practice holy virtues.

O my God, grant me love of You, hatred of myself, zeal for my neighbor, contempt of the world.

May I always obey my superiors, help my inferiors, be faithful to my friends, pardon my enemies.

May I overcome voluptuousness by austerity, avarice by liberality, anger by meekness, Luke warmness by fervor.

Make me prudent in my plans, constant in danger, patient in adversity, humble in prosperity.

Grant, O Lord, that I may be attentive in prayer, temperate in food, diligent in my duties, constant in my resolutions.

May I always be vigilant to dominate my nature, to cultivate grace, to observe the Commandments, to obtain eternal salvation.

O Lord, teach me the unimportance of this world, the greatness of divine things, the briefness of time, the duration of eternity.

Grant that I may always be prepared for death, that I may fear Your judgment, that I may escape hell, that I may merit Heaven. Amen

O My God, I want what You want, because You want it, as You want it, until You want it.

10c) MORMON

The Church of Jesus Christ of the Latter-Day Saints

Most LDS know the Lord's Prayer and use it as a model in how they address Deity; that they should express gratitude; that they may ask for help; and that this is the method for communicating with the Almighty God. Prayers are closed in the Lord's name as he is our Mediator to the Father.[101]

Seven Prayer Phrases for Mormons

Seven Clichéd Phrases from LDS Prayers

1. Thank thee for this day.
2. Thank thee for the moisture we have received.
3. Thank thee for all our many blessings.
4. Bless the refreshments to nourish and strengthen our bodies.
5. Bless that we can remember this lesson and apply it in our daily lives.
6. Bless those unable to attend that they will be here next week.
7. Bless that we will travel home in safety.[102]

Casting my Burdens on you O God

Father God, Thank you for your goodness and faithfulness in my life. Today I choose to cast my cares on you, I choose to release the weight of my burdens to you. Thank you for setting me free and aligning me to walk in victory in every areas of my life in Jesus' name. Amen![103]

10d) UNITARIAN

Giving Thanks for All good things to the Spirit of Life
I give thanks for the gift of awareness, which allows me to feel, think, and love. I give thanks for the smell of the rain, for the sight of each leaf of autumn, for the warm touch of a friend's hand, for the beautiful sounds of Bach, for the taste of an orange. I give thanks for the ability to think and act responsibly, knowing that my choices and actions affect myself and others. I give thanks for the ability to love and be loved, for the gift of friends and family. Spirit of Life, I give thanks for my awareness and precious gift of life.[104]

Unity

Today we open our awareness to the many profound blessings to our daily lives. We give thanks for the diverse ways in which God expresses through each of us and through our faith traditions. Oure paths are many, buy our spirit is one. Thank you, God, for our life, love, and wisdom for today and every day. We are unified in thought and purpose and inspired to take right action for the benefit of all humanity.[105]

10e) JEHOVAH WITNESSES

Proclamation Prayer to Jehovah God in Faithfulness
We pray to Jehovah God Maker of heaven and earth. We know that Jehovah is near all those who call upon him. We know that he will satisfy the desire of those who hear him; he hears their cry for help. We ask according to God's will. We ask for guidance in making wise decisions and for strength in coping with difficulties. We ask for guidance and strength through the Holy Spirit. We pray this through Jesus Christ. Amen.[106]

Living with Chronic Illness

The Bible's Answer.
the following three steps can help you cope:
Pray for strength to endure. (Phil 4:6,7)
Be positive. (Prov 17:22)
Build your hope in the future. (Rom 12:12)
Jw.org

According to biblical Christianity the name of GOD is YHWH, or understood as Yahweh or Jehovah. "God" aka "Heavenly Father" aka "Elohim" aka "Jehovah"

Quora.com

10f) JEWISH PRAYERS

Prayer for the hearing of Prayer

Hear our voice, O Lord our God; spare us and have mercy upon us, and accept our prayer in mercy and favor; for you are a God who hears and answers prayers and supplications; from your presence, O our King, turn us not away empty.

Prayer for healing

Heal us, O Lord, and we shall be healed; save us and we shall be saved; for you are our praise. Grant a perfect healing to all our wounds; [you may add a prayer for the sick here] for you, almighty King, are a faithful and merciful Physician. Blessed art thou O Lord, who heads the sick of your people Israel.

Prayer for Deliverance from Affliction

Look upon our affliction and plead our cause and redeem us speedily for your name's sake; for you are a mighty Redeemer.

Blessed art thou, O Lord, the Redeemer of Israel.

Grant Peace

Grant peace, welfare, blessing, grace, loving kindness and mercy unto us and unto all Israel, your people. Bless us, O our Father, even all of us together, with the light of your countenance; for by the light of your countenance you have given us, O Lord our God, the Torah of life, loving kindness and righteousness, blessing, mercy, life and peace; and may it be good in your sight to bless our people Israel at all times and in every hour with thy peace. Blessed are you, O Lord, who blesses your people Israel with peace.[107]

10g) ISLAM, MUSLIM PRAYERS

Peace

"In the name of God, The Merciful, The Compassionate, Peace Be Upon You."

For Any and Every Disease

O Allah, Lord of the people, remove all harm, give cure, for you are the one who cures. There is no curing except your curing – a curing that leaves no illness.[108]

Mercy and Forgiveness

Our lord! Allah! Open unto me the gates of thy mercy.

O Allah! Forgive me and turn to me: thou art most forgiving and Merciful.

O Allah! Beseech thee for forgiveness and for protection in this world and the world hereafter.[109]

10h) BUDDHISM

Be Well, Happy and Peaceful

May I be well, happy, and peaceful.
May my teachers be well, happy, and peaceful.
May my parents be well, happy, and peaceful.
May my relatives be well, happy, and peaceful.
May my friends be well, happy, and peaceful.
May the indifferent persons be well, happy, and peaceful.
May the unfriendly persons be well, happy, and peaceful.
May all meditators be well, happy, and peaceful.
May all beings be well, happy, and peaceful.[110]

Affliction Prayer

Ten Afflictions

1. greed,
2. anger,
3. delusion.
4. arrogance,
5. doubt,
6. wrong views.
7. perpetuity or cessation;
8. evil view of no causality;
9. inferior views;
10. observance of useless precepts, Ignorance of the truth is the root of all afflictions.[111]

The Eightfold Path
1. To have the highest view of Oneness of things.
2. To have the right thoughts of love and non-violence.
3. Use our speech – right way.
4. To perform the right actions (peaceful and moral).
5. To perform the right kind of work or livelihood.
6. To act with discipline and right effort.
7. To be mindful in – actions.
8. Meditate in the right way.[112]

10i) HINDUISM

Five Principles
1. God Exists: One Absolute
2. All human beings are divine
3. Unity of existence through love
4. Religious harmony
5. Knowledge of the Sacred River, Sacred Script, and the Sacred Mantra.

Ten Disciplines
1. Truth
2. Non-violence
3. Celibacy or non-adultery
4. No desire to possess or steal
5. Non-corrupt
6. Cleanliness
7. Contentment
8. Reading of scriptures
9. Austerity, Perseverance, Penance
10. 10. Regular prayers[113]

Peace

May peace be unto the heavens, unto the sky, and unto the earth. May peace be unto the water, unto the herbs, and unto the trees.[104]

Prayer for All Aspects of Life

O All Powerful God.
you are the protector of the whole physical creation.
May you protect my body. you are the source of all life. you are the source of all strength. May though make me strong. O, omnipotent Lord, I live to thee to fill up all my wants and to give me perfection, physical, mental, and spiritual.

11

THE LORD'S PRAYER

Also Called: THE OUR FATHER

The Lord's Prayer
It is said that Jesus prayed to his Father in heaven often. He also was asked by his disciples how to pray.

He responded this is how you are to pray:
Our Father, who art in heaven, hallowed be thy name; thy kingdom come, thy will be done on earth as it is in heaven. Give us this day our daily bread, and forgive us our trespasses, as we forgive those who trespass against us; and lead us not into temptation, but deliver us from evil.[114]

Our Father in heaven, hallowed be your name, your kingdom come, your will be done, on earth as in heaven. Give us today our daily bread; and forgive us our debts, as we forgive our debtors; and do not subject us to the final test, but deliver us from the evil one. *(Mt 6:9-13)*

The Lord's Prayer *(Expanded Version)*

Our Father who art in heaven
  May we dwell with you in heaven forever and ever

Hallowed be thy name
  May we praise thy holy name forever and ever

thy kingdom come
  May we help bring your holy love to others

thy will be done on earth as it is in heaven
  May we help accomplish your holy good with love

Give us this day our daily bread
  May we receive the Word of God every day

And forgive us our trespasses
  May we receive your mercy and forgiveness

As we forgive those who trespass against us
  May we forgive others always with your mercy

And lead us not into temptation
  May we do good during trials and tribulations

But deliver us from evil
  May we receive your guidance, grace, and love[115]

THE LORD'S PRAYER – Seven Petitions Explained

This information is a teaching on The Seven Petitions:

"In the Our Father, the object of the first three petitions is the glory of the Father: the sanctification of his name, the coming of the kingdom, and the fulfillment of his will. The four others present our wants to him: they ask that our lives be nourished, healed of sin, and made victorious in the struggle of good over evil."[116]

1. *Hallowed Be thy Name*

The first petition is to take a closer look at the word hallowed says Holy, with Sacred Veneration." We are to know that this reference is pertaining to his holiness; God is complete holiness. Within the scriptures it says that God revealed his name to Moses as "I AM." As the history of God and his People unfolded other names were used to refer to God: Lord, Shepherd, and King were a few. Further revelation through his Son Jesus Christ, taught us that God is Our Father.

2. *Thy Kingdom Come*

In the second petition, we pray that "thy Kingdom Come" promised by God. The kingdom was here already with the presence of Christ (during his life, death, and resurrection). Now we look for kingdom of love, peace, and mercy. We look for the forgiveness of our sins and to be fully reconciled with God. At the same time, it is not here fully because we are not fully transformed into our heavenly selves.

3. *Thy Will Be Done on Earth as It Is in heaven*

In this third petition, we want his will to be done to fulfill God's plan. In Luke it says, "Not my will but yours be done." We pray to be united with our Father, Son, and Holy Spirit; on Earth as it is in heaven.[117]

4. Give Us This Day Our Daily Bread

Our daily bread can refer to a number of items: our nourishment, the word of God, or the Body of Christ (Holy Communion). Another item to consider is that the Bread of Life is Jesus Christ himself.

5. Forgive Us Our Trespasses as We Forgive Those Who Trespass Against Us

We ask the Father to forgive us. Just as we need to be merciful to obtain mercy. Jesus taught us to forgive others; even to forgive our enemies. Jesus is our example asking the Father to forgive those who crucified him.

6. And Lead Us Not into Temptation

We are not tempted from God who is all goodness and love; he tempts no one. We ask God not to allow us to be tempted or into a path of sinfulness. Jesus was sent to cleanse us and to die on the cross for our sins. We now entrust ourselves into the hands of the Holy Spirit to lead us and guide us to righteousness.

7.   But Deliver Us from Evil

We pray with the rest of the Body of Christ, with the rest of the church for God to deliver us from evil. The victory that Christ has already won over evil. The evil we ask God to protect us from is not just an idea, but it is Satan, the fallen angel who wants to prevent our salvation.[118]

> Rise early in the morning,
> go to a deserted place and pray.
> *(see Mk 1:35)*

APPENDIX A

HOW TO IMPROVE YOUR PRAYER LIFE

FIVE RECOMMENDATIONS

Our prayer is not our quest for God, but God's quest for us. Once seen the primacy of grace, it's God's addressing of us. What is right and true in us, it's the Holy Spirit prompting us to pray for what He wants to give us already. Prayer is a conversation among friends.

1. **Take the time to Pray** – Take time each day to converse with God. A dedicated time of prayer can help tremendously in improving your prayer life.
2. **Finding the Center** – Prayer helps us to find the center; it puts us into the here and now where we are being molded by God. The still point that the whole of your life should revolve around. A saint is someone who prays, who regularly prays and has found his center still point.
3. **Pray with Honesty** – Be honest and clear when you pray. Do not hold back unpleasant subjects such as troubles, guilt, sin, confusion, anger, frustration, etc.
4. **Listen attentively** – This conversation takes the prayer life from one-way to two-way communication. We include a listening aspect with our prayer life. This may be done

when reading scripture, speaking to someone, or listening to your interior consciousness, whether feeling desolation or consolation. You are reflecting and meditating on events, situations, people, your inner thoughts and God speaking to you about all things of you and your life. These feelings may be God speaking through these moments, working through your feelings. *(Have you ever imagined what Jesus would say to you about a question if you asked?) {scripture-based A possible discernment}*

5. **Silence** – Sometimes we stay so engaged and busy we lack silence. We need to bring silence into our everyday busy lives *(like the Holy Hour in front of the Blessed Sacrament, or pray the Jesus Prayer P105)*. We seek the good that is absent and rest in it once it is found. Savoring in the good of God is a silencing effect which is a good aspect and key to prayer. Silence allows us to listen and to pray.

These are five actions that can assist one to improve your prayer life. As I have just reflected - it is our communication to God and hearing what He has to tell us, not the other way around. In prayer we seek someone greater than ourselves. We seek someone better than ourselves. We seek someone to emulate; someone to learn from. In other words, our will seeks the good that is absent and savors it when it is found.

Reference: Bishop Robert Barron, The Word on Fire, Video from YouTube, <u>*Bishop Barron on Prayer*</u>

APPENDIX B

THE IMITATION OF CHRIST
(IV BOOKS)

This little book is a gem: "The Imitation of Christ." There is knowledge, understanding, and wisdom within its pages. This book was written over five centuries ago and is still published to this day. Below are some prayers from chapters; gems of knowledge and wisdom that will help one become closer to God and Imitate the Son of God.

Over a ten-year period, I read, underlined, and took notes. I've added some of the prayers in this Appendix (find this book, it will change your life). I believe that this book is of great benefit to anyone who incorporates the principles into their being. *(Some of the words here are verbatim and others are paraphrased).*

Bk III Ch3, **listen to God's words humbly, not lightly**
Help me, O Lord, always to listen to your word and to accept it. May all my thoughts, words, and actions be based on your word. Amen.

Bk III Ch19, **support of injuries proves true patience**
O my God, may your grace make me capable of doing what my corrupt nature thinks difficult or impossible. Infuse in me the virtue of patience. Amen.

Bk III Ch43, **against useless, worldly learning**
Invite me, Lord, to attend your school: Make me simple and docile as a child, so that I may learn your divine science and love you with all my mind, will, and heart. Amen.

Bk III Ch46, **confidence in God when criticized**
O Lord God, just Judge, you know the fragility and malice of men. Therefore, be my strength and my hope. Mercifully grant me your pardon for all the times I have foiled to follow your counsel and advice. Amen.

Bk III Ch56, **deny self and Imitate Christ carrying the cross**
O my Redeemer. my crucified Christ, grant me the grace to live and die happily in the shadow of the cross, because you saved me by your holy death on the cross. Amen.

Bk III Ch57, **do not be dejected when you fall into defects**
O Lord, do not abandon me in time of adversity or when I sin, but uphold me with your grace and mercy. I ask this grace with humility and constancy, and I am sure of obtaining it from your infinite mercy. Amen.

Bk III Ch59, **center all hope and confidence in God alone**
O Lord, comfort us in our affliction, strengthen us in our trials, defend us in perils, save us from our enemies. You are our God, Father and Savior. Help us, therefore, so that we may not perish, but will attain eternal salvation. Amen.

Infuse me with thy love.

APPENDIX C

FAVORITE SCRIPTURES

† *(cf. Heb 13:8) Jesus Christ is the same yesterday, today, and forever.*

At Easter, we rejoice because Christ did not remain in the tomb, his body did not see corruption; he belongs to the world of the living, not to the world of the dead; we rejoice because he is the Alpha and also the Omega, as we proclaim in the rite of the Paschal Candle; *he lives not only yesterday, but today and for eternity.*[119]

† *(cf. Gal 2:20) It is no longer I who live, but Christ who lives in me.*

I think that what happens in Baptism can be more easily explained for us if we consider the final part of the short spiritual autobiography that Saint Paul gave us in his Letter to the Galatians. Its concluding words contain the heart of this biography: *"It is no longer I who live, but Christ who lives in me."* I live, but I am no longer I. The "I," the essential identity of man – of this man, Paul – has been changed. He still exists, and he no longer exists. He has passed through a "not" and he now finds himself continually in this "not": I, but no longer I.[119]

† *(cf. Gal 3:28) You have become one in Christ.*

Paul explains the same thing to us once again from another angle when, in Chapter Three of the Letter to the Galatians, he speaks of the "promise," saying that it was given to an individual–to one person: to Christ. He alone carries within himself the whole "promise." But what then happens with us? Paul answers: *You have become one in Christ.* Not just one thing, but one, one only, one single new subject. This liberation of our "I" from its isolation, this finding oneself in a new subject means finding oneself within the vastness of God and being drawn into a life which has now moved out of the context of "dying and becoming."[119]

† *(cf. Jn 14:19) I live and you will live also,*

"I live and you will live also," says Jesus to his disciples, that is, to us. We will live through our existential communion with him, through being taken up into him who is life itself. Eternal life, blessed immortality, we have not by ourselves or in ourselves, but through a relation – through existential communion with him who is Truth and Love and is therefore eternal: God himself. Simple indestructibility of the soul by itself could not give meaning to eternal life, it could not make it a true life. Life comes to us from being loved by him who is Life; it comes to us from living-with and loving-with him. I, but no longer I: this is the way of the Cross, the way that "crosses over" a life simply closed in on the I, thereby opening up the road towards true and lasting joy.[119]

† *(see Acts 1:8) When the holy Spirit comes upon you, you will be my witnesses to the ends of the earth.*

When we receive the Holy Spirit, the Paraclete, we have the truthsayer within us. The one that will tell us what God wants and always the truth. We are called to speak the truth when we are called, inspired, and lead.[120]

† *(see Jn 13:34a) I give you a new commandment: love one another. As I have loved you.*

The 2 commandments that Jesus expresses, if followed are all anyone needs to follow because they resolve all others, even the 613 Mosaic laws of the Jews and fulfill the 10 commandments. This new commandment wasn't new but new to them, it was from the old testament Leviticus 19:18. Puts Jesus on a par with God. The saying 'love conquers all' is true.

"You shall love the Lord, your God, with all your heart, with all your soul, and with all your mind. This is the greatest and the first commandment. The second is like it: You shall love your neighbor as yourself. The whole law and the prophets depend on these two commandments." (Mt 22:36-40)[120]

† *(see 1 Pet 2:9) You are "a chosen race, a royal priesthood, a holy nation, a people of his own, so that you may announce the praises" of him who called you out of darkness into his wonderful light.*

The Apostle Peter wanted to encourage and uplift the disciples: because of them thinking that God had abandoned them from hardships and persecutions. Peter wrote to encourage them, offering them hope and meaning in the midst of their suffering; so that they realize God called them out of their darkness into His light.[120]

† *(Isa 49:6) I will make you a light to the nations, that my salvation may reach to the ends of the earth.*

This prophesy was fulfilled in Jesus. *(Lk 2:25-32)* Simeon, a righteous and devout man, awaited the consolation of Israel. When he saw Jesus, he held him and said, "Now, Master, you may let your servant go (Simeon meant himself) in peace, according to your word, for my eyes have seen your salvation, which you prepared in sight of all the peoples, a light for revelation to the Gentiles, and glory for your people Israel." A prophesy that unfolded as it was told.[120]

† *(Lk 4:18-19) "The Spirit of the Lord is upon me, because he has anointed me to bring glad tidings to the poor. He has sent me to proclaim liberty to captives and recovery of sight to the blind, to let the oppressed go free, and to proclaim a year acceptable to the Lord."*

This is a beautiful fulfilment of scripture. Jesus (as an adult) read this scripture in the synagogue and when sat back down he said, "Today this scripture passage is fulfilled in your hearing." He was so precise, to follow all of his Father's will, that all would be done that had been told. All promises met.[120]

† *(Jn 14:6) Jesus said to him, "I am the way and the truth and the life. No one comes to the Father except through me.*

The meaning of this is not complicated. We are called to imitate Jesus because he is the only <u>way</u> to follow, all that Jesus is, has and will always be <u>truth</u>, Jesus' <u>life</u> is exemplary and we must imitate him. He is love and compassion for all. We are to become like Jesus the righteous one. Thus, as he enters Heaven, our hope is to become so much like him, it is not I who lives, but Jesus within me who lives. Therefore, I must die to myself so Jesus may live within. I aspire to become better and better each day.[120]

† *(Mt 10:32) Everyone who acknowledges me before others I will acknowledge before my heavenly Father.*

What a wonderful thing. To be in a place and feeling insecure or feeling alone and alienated, then the leader or King stands up and acknowledges you as his friend, now that would be a great day. We must remember, He is King of the Kingdom we are in right now. He has already acknowledged us first. Keep what has been given is to take care of it and help grow what has been given. Never deny your friend.[120]

† *(Isa 55:11) So shall my word be that goes forth from my mouth; It shall not return to me empty, but shall do what pleases me, achieving the end for which I sent it.*

God who knows all things does nothing without knowing the outcome. Know this, every word spoken to you is meant for you and is not a coincidence.[120]

† *(Lk 1:37) For nothing will be impossible for God.*

In context from Gabriel the Archangel is reassuring Mary that she can be the handmaiden of the Lord. God, the creator of the Earth & the Universe can accomplish anything. So the virginity of Mary can be overcome by God.[121]

† *(1 Jn 5:17) All wrongdoing is sin, but there is sin that is not deadly.*

If we see someone sin, we can pray for them or they can if not a deadly sin and God will give them life. We must stay aware of our God and trust in Him. He is the only one that knows the future and He loves us. We should know God's will and pray for it and His grace to be sheltered by Him. Stay righteous and live in Him.

† *(Mt 5:14) You are the light of the world.*

This scripture helps one to realize that they should share what they see. It refers to a biblical reading is meant not for oneself but meant for sharing. This light we shed illuminates God's way, truth, and life; is the good news of Jesus Christ! There is love and mercy for each of us, that leads to eternal life and union with God.[122]

† *(Mt 5:1-12)* The Sermon on the Mount. *(The Beatitudes)*

When he saw the crowds, he went up the mountain, and after he had sat down, his disciples came to him. He began to teach them, saying:

Blessed are the poor in spirit,
for theirs is the kingdom of heaven.

Blessed are they who mourn,
for they will be comforted.

Blessed are the meek,
for they will inherit the land.

Blessed are they who hunger and thirst for righteousness,
for they will be satisfied.

Blessed are the merciful,
for they will be shown mercy.

Blessed are the clean of heart,
for they will see God.

*Blessed are the peacemakers,
for they will be called children of God.*

*Blessed are they who are persecuted for the sake of righteousness,
for theirs is the kingdom of heaven.*

Blessed are you when they insult you and persecute you and utter every kind of evil against you because of me. Rejoice and be glad, for your reward will be great in heaven. Thus, they persecuted the prophets who were before you.

How beautiful and soothing is the heart of our God. How Jesus reveals it so carefully by words that mean so much to the downtrodden and sheep that are lost or turned away. These blessings are feelings to remember when we live each moment. Live your day in the present and worry no more of your past, but know your future is only dependent on the present.[120]

† *(Mt 5:42) Give to the one who asks of you, and do not turn your back on one who wants to borrow.*

We must help someone who asks for something. We've been given all that we own and all that we are. Share all that is from God.[120]

† *(Mt 5:44) But I say to you, love your enemies, and pray for those who persecute you.*

This Christianity saying is contrary to the way of the world. As a Christian we are called to become Christ-like. God is the Creator of all and loves all. We are all made in the image and likeness of God. Therefore, we are to love all, and participate in the divine life. Yes, even to the point of loving your enemies, and praying for those who persecute you.¹²²

† (Rom 12:1-2) *I urge you therefore, brothers, by the mercies of God, to offer your bodies as a living sacrifice, holy and pleasing to God, your spiritual worship. Do not conform yourselves to this age but be transformed by the renewal of your mind, that you may discern what is the will of God, what is good and pleasing and perfect.*¹²⁰

Here we are called to move away from the Mosaic Laws, in our time, they are examples of cultic superstitions, and misdirected sacrifices. We are called to sacrifice for each other, using our abilities to help each other. To assist them, God distributes a variety of gifts to the fellowship of believers, including those of prophecy, teaching, and exhortation. Whether we are skilled with an ability of strength or mind to offer it as a sacrifice for God's use, and his Children.

† (Phil 4:8) *Finally, brothers, whatever is true, whatever is honorable, whatever is just, whatever is pure, whatever is lovely, whatever is gracious, if there is any excellence and if there is anything worthy of praise, think about these things.*

Although the language employs terms from Roman Stoic thought. To follow Paul's lead, we are to seek all good things to Rejoice in the Lord always, again, Rejoice in the Lord always. Oh, how extremely necessary for me is your grace, O Lord, so that I might begin what is good and go forward with it until I fulfill it! For just as without it I can do nothing, so I can do all things in you, when your grace strengthens me. O, truly the grace of heaven! Our merits are nonexistent without it and the gifts of nature are worthless. Without grace, O Lord, the arts, riches, beauty, strength, genius, and eloquence, are all without value in your sight. Help us Lord that we find grace in all things for all things came from you and were good.[120]

† *(1 Cor 3:9) We are God's co-workers.*

Though often unconscious collaborators with God's will, we can also enter deliberately into the divine plan by our actions, prayers and sufferings. We then fully become "God's fellow workers" and co-workers for his kingdom.

† *(Jn 6:29) Jesus said to them, this is the work of God, that you believe in the one he sent.*

Jesus performed miracles and wondrous signs to the ones that God had sent him and that received the grace of faith. He did this so that all would believe that He was sent from God and 'is the Son of God.' When He called God, Father, He established a new relationship with humanity. God, thru divine providence and continued revelation brings our knowledge to levels that are understandable for humanity as we evolve.[122]

† *(1 Cor 2:16b) Have the mind of Christ.*

Since spiritual persons have been given knowledge of what pertains to God, they share in God's own capacity to judge. One to whom the mind of the Lord and of Christ is revealed can be said to share in some sense in God's exemption from counseling and criticism. The doctrine of original sin is, so to speak, the "reverse side" of the Good News that Jesus is the Savior of all men, that all need salvation and that salvation is offered to all through Christ. The Church, which has the mind of Christ, knows very well that we cannot tamper with the revelation of original sin without undermining the mystery of Christ.[123]

† *(Eph 6:12) For our struggle is not with flesh and blood but with the principalities, with the powers, with the world rulers of this present darkness, with the evil spirits in the heavens.*

Dictators, Princes of this world (that are of this world), the world rulers to control the world following all for personal gain of mind and matter. They hear the darkness and follow what gains them in pleasure and their gain. The darkness and evil spirits surround us and feed all those that will hear and anyone they can suey. God's angels, spirits, and heaven's power continue to maintain rule over them to prevent action that is outside of what God's will allows. Our angels protect us and use God's power and His will to fight the demonic demons and hold in check the prince of this world Satan.

Let us pray unceasingly to ask for God's grace and protection until Jesus returns. The invisible veil that protects us from the frightful evil that surrounds us all. Our angels constantly fighting the ones that fly around to devour all that stand with the Trinity and Imitate Jesus that showed us the way.[120]

REFERENCES

The New American Bible (Rev. Ed.) NABRE reference used unless listed.

1. Laudate App, The Passion and Interior Solitude
2. The Word Among Us, Jan/Feb 2018
3. Ps 118:24
4. *see* Lk 18:13b
5. *see* Lev 19:18b, *cf.* Mk 12:31, *cf.* Mt 19:19b
6. *see* Mt 6:14a
7. *see* Lk 22:42
8. *see* Gal 2:20
9. *see* Ps 91:11
10. *see* Rom 10:13
11. *cf.* Rom 10:9
12. *cf.* Jn 3:16
13. *ref* Miles Christi #46
14. *see* 1 Cor 13:4a, *see* Mt 6:14, *see* Gal 5:22-23, *see* Rom 5:5, Jn 14:6a

15. Karl Paul Reinhold Niebuhr

16. *see* Ps 138

17. *see* Ps 90

18. *see* Eph 6:18, *see* Rom 5a, *see* 1 Jn 4:7, *see* Jas 1:2-4, *see* Jas 5, *see* The Imitation of Christ Bk3, Ch24

19. *see* Ps 81

20. *see* Isa 53

21. *see* Prov 3:26-34

22. *see* Ps 34

23. *see* Ps 118, 136

24. *see* Ps 147

25. *see* Psalms 34, 46, 145 and *see* Isaiah 49

26. 26. Ps 37:3-4, 23, 39

27. 27. Three Values, Unity, Dignity, and Work, March 22, 2016, Archbishop Bernardino Auza

28. *see* Isaiah 53

29. Prayer and Temperament, Different Prayer Forms for Different Personality Types; Chester P. Michael, Marie C. Norrisey

30. Prayer and Temperament, Different Prayer Forms for Different Personality Types; Chester P. Michael, Marie C. Norrisey

31. Prayer and Temperament, Different Prayer Forms for Different Personality Types; Chester P. Michael, Marie C. Norrisey

32. Prayer and Temperament, Different Prayer Forms for Different Personality Types; Chester P. Michael, Marie C. Norrisey

33. Prayer and Temperament, Different Prayer Forms for Different Personality Types; Chester P. Michael, Marie C. Norrisey

34. Litany of the Holy Spirit by Richard Rohr, 'The Naked Now'

35. Ann Spangler, A Litany of Hebrew names and titles of God.

36. Mt 5:1-12

37. Harry Dudley SCE, (ref. Laudate app)

38. Rom 8:25-27

39. Inspired by Jane Craft

40. Jn 3:16

41. St. Mother Teresa of Calcutta

42. 1 Sam 3:9

43. St. John Damascus

44. St. Francis of Assisi

45. Isa 50:7

46. Rom 8:28

47. Acts 9:10

48. Isa 6:8

49. St. Maria Faustina

50. Mt 25:21

51. St. Augustine

52. Jn 13:34a

53. St. Augustine

54. St. Francis of Assisi

55. Joan of Arc, *(The Life of Joan of Arc (1909) by Anatole France)*

56. St. Teresa of Ávila

57. St. Alfonso Liguori

58. Jn 8:29a

59. *see* Jn 5:25b

60. Isa 49:13b

61. Mt 28:20b

62. Ps 7:2, NAB

63. St. Maria Faustina

64. Num 6:24-26

65. Prayer of St. Francis of Assisi

66. Acts 2:38

67. Prayer of St. John of the Cross

68. St. Mother Teresa of Calcutta

69. St. Thomas Aquinas

70. St. Augustine of Hippo, www.catholic.org/prayers

71. Act of Offering #1/www.catholic.org/prayers

72. Saint Ignatius of Loyola

73. Saint Francis de Sales

74. St. Thomas Aquinas

75. St. John Vianney

76. *see* St. Thomas Aquinas
77. Inspired by Dom William
78. Rom 8:31b
79. St. Francis of Assisi
80. www.lastwordeulogies.com
81. www.lastwordeulogies.com/Modified from Christian prayers III & VIII
82. TD Jakes
83. Jer 17:5-11
84. *see* Ps 31
85. *see* Isa 44 and Ps 23
86. Ps 37: 3-6, 23-24, 39-40
87. Ps 118
88. *see* Mt 22:37
89. *see* Lk 10:27 & Deut. 6:5
90. *see* Deut. 30:6
91. *see* Deut. 10:12
92. see Mt 11:28-30
93. *ref.* Bishop William E. Lori., Columbia Mag., June 2011
94. St. Ignatius of Loyola
95. United States Catholic Catechism for Adults, United States Conference of Catholic Bishops

96. St. Ignatius of Loyola
97. *ref* Miles Christi #45
98. www.catholic.org/prayers
99. United States Catholic Catechism for Adults, United States Conference of Catholic Bishops
100. Handbook for Chaplains: Comfort My People, Mary M. Toole
101. Quora.com
102. LDS Living.com
103. Famous Lds Quotes Prayer. QuotesGram
104. Chaplain Services
105. Chaplain Services
106. JW.org
107. Sabbath Amidah/Zion CS
108. Handbook for Chaplains: Comfort My People, Mary M. Toole
109. Muslim-Prayers .com
110. wikihow.com
111. sutrasmantras.info
112. Handbook for Chaplains: Comfort My People, Mary M. Toole
113. Hinduism.about.com
114. Mt 6:9-13
115. Mt 6:9
116. Catechism of the Catholic Church, CCC #2857

REFERENCES

117. *see* Catechism of the Catholic Church, no.2860

118. *see* Catechism of the Catholic Church, no.2864

119. Pope Benedict XVI / p132

120. Al Mozingo / John Oliver Kleine Jr.Gospel of Luke Commentary, Ignatius Catholic Study Bible

121. The Word on Fire Bible (The Gospels) Bishop Robert Barron

122. www.biblegateway.com (footnotes 1 Cor i), CCC 389

Reference All Your Actions with Jesus.

www.ingramcontent.com/pod-product-compliance
Ingram Content Group UK Ltd.
Pitfield, Milton Keynes, MK11 3LW, UK
UKHW022215230426
12048UKWH00016BA/853